D0050627

PRAISE FOR *PEAK PERFORMANCE*:

"So much in this book resonates with me. With practical advice
for performance in the workplace or on the playing field, Brad and Steve
meticulously deliver a comprehensive understanding of
peak performance and how to achieve it."

—*Dick Costolo, CEO of Chorus, former CEO of Twitter*

"Brad Stulberg is one of my favorite writers about two of my favorite topics:
physical and mental performance. This book brings them together."

—*Ryan Holiday, bestselling author of* The Obstacle is the Way
and Ego is the Enemy

"Tackling the mysteries of human optimization with science and insight from
some of the world's greatest athletes, artists, and intellectuals, *Peak Performance*
provides the roadmap you need to transcend your limitations, unleash your
inner greatness, and, most importantly, sustain it over time. An absolute must
read for anyone interested in unlocking the potential to become your best self!"

—*Rich Roll, author of* Finding Ultra *and* The Plantpower Way

"Brad Stulberg is one of the most gifted science writers of our times,
a master at translating fascinating findings into concrete strategies.
Peak Performance provides actionable insights from the cutting-edge research
on how people excel. This book will be a must-read for anyone who wants to up
their game, transcend their boundaries, and get out of their comfort zone."

—*Kelly McGonigal, Stanford psychology instructor and author of*
The Willpower Instinct *and* The Upside of Stress

"What do great artists, champion athletes, and brilliant researchers
have in common? More than you'd expect, as Brad Stulberg and Steve Magness
reveal in this magnificent silo-breaking synthesis of the hidden patterns
that enable great performance across disciplines."

—*Alex Hutchinson, Runner's World "Sweat Science" columnist and
author of* What Comes First: Cardio or Weights?

"*Peak Performance* is a must read for anyone hoping to grow and achieve success in any area of their life. Relatable and readable, it identifies the skills and disciplines successful people have in common and teaches us what we can do to achieve the success that we want. I am excited to put what I have learned to use in my running and beyond."

—*Kara Goucher, two-time Olympic marathoner*

"Full of inspiration and information, *Peak Performance* is a must-read for anyone dedicated to self-optimization. I will be reading and re-reading this book for years to come."

—*Matt Billingslea, drummer, Taylor Swift Band*

"Brad and Steve uncover secrets of the world's best performers to help us all become more effective in our own pursuits. *Peak Performance* is a must read for everyone: from athletes to artists, and certainly entrepreneurs. Basically, this book is for anyone looking to take their skills to the next level."

—*Dr. Bob Kocher, partner at Venrock Capital, consulting professor at Stanford School of Medicine, formerly special assistant to the President of the United States on Health Care*

"We all wonder why some people become great successes and others do not. It seems a mystery. However, *Peak Performance* presents the science that illuminates the common practices of game changers, and most importantly, shows us how we can benefit from applying them in our own lives."

—*David Goss, professor emeritus of mathematics at The Ohio State University*

"As I read *Peak Performance* I found myself amazed that there is actually science to back up what I have found true as I sought to maximize my abilities throughout my professional running career. The reader is sure to be perplexed by Brad and Steve's surprising findings and empowered to make some changes to their competitive mentality so they can achieve their own peak performance."

—*Ryan Hall, United States half-marathon record holder*

"*Peak Performance* deeply explores the cycle of intense creativity that remains a mysterious realm even to myself—despite my best efforts to mine it for all it's worth. I think it's clear that Stulberg and Magness are really onto something here."

—*Emil Alzamora, internationally-acclaimed sculptor*

PE∧K
PERFORMANCE

ALSO BY STEVE MAGNESS:

The Science of Running

ELEVATE YOUR GAME,
AVOID BURNOUT,
AND THRIVE WITH
THE NEW SCIENCE
OF SUCCESS

PEΛK
PERFORMANCE

BRAD
STULBERG

STEVE
MAGNESS

RODALE.

RODALE *wellness*

Live happy. Be healthy. Get inspired.

Sign up today to get exclusive access to our authors, exclusive bonuses, and the most authoritative, useful, and cutting-edge information on health, wellness, fitness, and living your life to the fullest.

Visit us online at RodaleWellness.com
Join us at RodaleWellness.com/Join

Rodale books may be purchased for business or promotional use or for special sales. For information, please write to: Special Markets Department, Rodale, Inc., 733 Third Avenue, New York, NY 10017

Printed in the United States of America

Rodale Inc. makes every effort to use acid-free ♾, recycled paper ♻.

Book design by Christina Gaugler

Illustrations by Willie Ryan

Library of Congress Cataloging-in-Publication Data is on file with the publisher.

ISBN: 978-1-62336-793-0 hardcover

Distributed to the trade by Macmillan

4 6 8 10 9 7 5   hardcover

 **RODALE.**

We inspire health, healing, happiness, and love in the world.
Starting with you.

To Caitlin, Mom, Dad, Lois, and Eric

To Mom, Dad, Emily, and Phillip

And to all the researchers and great performers whose brilliant work makes up the foundation of this book. Thank you for giving us the pieces to put together.

CONTENTS

FOREWORD

Is Healthy, Sustainable Peak Performance Possible?

In the summer of 2003, a precocious 18-year-old sat nervously on a grass field flanked by eight lanes of a warmup track, awaiting the final call to the starting line. This wasn't your ordinary high school track meet, or even a state championship; this was the Prefontaine Classic, the crown jewel of track-and-field. A few days earlier, the same 18-year-old was sitting in his physics class thinking about his high school crush, Amanda. Now, he was sitting amidst the best runners in the world, wondering how he'd measure up in the sport's preeminent event—the mile.

As he watched stars such as Olympic medalist Bernard Lagat execute their intricate prerace rituals, he tried to distract himself by playing his Game Boy; he stuck out like a sore thumb. A few long minutes later, when the athletes were summoned from the warmup area to the starting line, he was forced to leave the comfort of the video game *Super Mario Bros.* In a futile attempt to stay calm while entering the packed Hayward Field, located on the campus of the University of Oregon—a running mecca if there ever was one—he kept repeating the mantra, "Don't look up, don't look up." The top of his head, not his face, was broadcast across the country, live on NBC. Before he could process that he was lining up next to Kevin Sullivan, who had placed fifth at the previous Olympics, his name was suddenly belted out over the loud speaker. Any illusion of calm was shattered. A wave of anxiety coursed through his body. Whatever little food was in his stomach rose into his chest. "Shit. Here we go," he thought, as the starter raised his gun. "Just don't puke."

Four minutes and 1 second later, it was all over. In that short time, he had become the sixth fastest high school miler in the history of the United States, the then-fastest high school miler in the country, and the fifth fastest junior in the world. He had gone toe-to-toe with collegiate superstar Alan Webb, who had a 3:53 mile to his credit and who would eventually set the American record of 3:46. He finished within arm's reach of Olympian Michael Stember and passed the then–US mile champion Seneca Lassiter, who promptly dropped out of the race after the high school kid left him in the dust on the final lap. In other words, he had officially become a teenage prodigy.

Even so, the disappointment that came with finishing just shy of the sport's magical 4-minute mile was evident. When the official results were announced, the NBC broadcast showed a wiry, completely depleted kid, hands covering his face. As the initial flood of emotion wore off, however, he couldn't help but revel in a bit of hard-earned contentedness. He thought to himself, "I'm 18 years old and running in the biggest professional meet in the country; breaking 4 minutes will soon be an after-thought."

NBC's color commentators were cooing over the performance of the high school kid. "You got to say something about a kid who can stay that disciplined," they remarked. If only they knew.

REACHING THIS LEVEL of performance demanded more than just talent and hard work. Ask those who knew him and a single descriptor invariably came to mind: obsessive. It was the only word that fit. Friends and family repeated this word so often that it could have easily been dismissed as trite and cliché. Except it wasn't.

His days were a monotonous pursuit of excellence. Wake up at 6 a.m., head out the door for a 9-mile run, go to school, lift weights, and then run another 9 miles at 6 p.m. In order to avoid injury and illness, he adhered to a rigid diet and religiously went to bed hours before his peers. His life was an exercise in willpower and self-control.

He insisted on sticking to his training plan always, even if that meant running 100 miles during a week-long cruise vacation—circling the 160-meter track on the top deck until not fatigue but dizziness stopped him. He ran through tropical storms, summer heat advisories, and family emergencies. No natural or human disaster could prevent him from getting a workout in. One more example of his obsession manifested itself in his love life, or lack thereof. Apologies are long overdue for the unfortunate girlfriend with whom he cut things off simply because his racing had gone south during their courtship, even though she, of course, had nothing to do with it. His obsession surfaced every weekend when he regularly chose his 10 p.m. bedtime over parties and opportunities to meet girls. In other words, he was far from your average high school boy, but then again, average high school boys don't run 4-minute miles. He had the rage to master: an unending, unrelenting resolve to do everything he could to reach his goals. And it was paying off.

He was one of the fastest documented 18-year-olds on the planet and one of the fastest high school runners in the history of the sport. He received recruiting letters from nearly every university in the country, ranging from athletic powerhouses like Oregon to bastions of academic prowess like Harvard. His dreams were filled with Olympic rings, medals, and thoughts of conquering the world. And they were all realistic.

A FEW YEARS LATER, across the country in Washington, DC, a young man was preparing for his first day at a new job. He hurried out the door after his usual morning hygiene routine—brush teeth, shave, shower, get dressed, and go—a routine he'd condensed into 12 minutes. His morning routine hadn't always been such a sprint. But after 2 years of working at the elite consulting firm McKinsey & Company, he'd applied to his own life the uncanny efficiency that he'd helped Fortune 500 companies achieve. No waste. No downtime. Completely streamlined. The sole pitfall of his uber-efficient mornings was that it caused him to sweat, which was only exacerbated by a tight-fitting suit and the thick humidity of summer in Washington, DC.

A single thought dominated the first 10 minutes of his walk to work: stop sweating. He wasn't accustomed to the suit, which was a step up in dress code required by the new job. He'd have to alter his morning routine: either build in more time or lower the water temperature in the shower. Maybe both. He was good at this kind of analytical thinking. In the months prior, he built a model that projected the economic impact of United States health care reform, a sweeping and messy legislation that would shake up multiple industries. His model had made its way around the Beltway, and experts, most of whom were twice his age, agreed it was pretty damn good. It undoubtedly helped him land his new gig.

When he turned onto Pennsylvania Avenue, however, his thoughts shifted away from which variable of his morning routine he'd alter first. "Holy shit," he thought, "this is awesome," as he arrived at number 1600, the White House. There, he'd be working for the prestigious National Economic Council, helping to advise the president of the United States on health care.

LIKE MOST EXCEPTIONAL PERFORMERS, this young professional's journey to the White House was rooted in a combination of good DNA and hard work. He scored highly on an early childhood IQ test, but not off the charts: His verbal intelligence was exceptional, but his mathematical ability and spatial skills were quite ordinary, if that. He worked his ass off in school, regularly choosing to immerse himself in philosophy, economics, and psychology rather than in booze and parties. Though he was good enough to play small-school collegiate football, he instead chose to attend the University of Michigan and focus singularly on academics.

His scholarly success attracted recruiters from the prestigious consulting firm McKinsey & Company. At McKinsey, he quickly earned a reputation as a top performer. In whatever time remained at the end of his 70-plus-hour workweeks, he practiced his presentation skills and read the *Wall Street Journal*, the *Harvard Business Review*, and countless economics books. His friends often joked that he was "anti-fun." No doubt he was grinding, but he was enjoying it, too.

His performance at McKinsey soared on an upward trajectory, and he got staffed on increasingly high-profile projects: It wasn't long before he was counseling the CEOs of multibillion-dollar companies. That's when, in the winter of 2010, he was asked to build the previously mentioned model that would forecast the effects of United States health care reform, a herculean task. Imagine being confronted with 50 variables, all of which interact with one another and none of which is certain, and then being asked: "Tell us what is going to happen, and do it on this spreadsheet."

He dug in and worked harder than ever before. If he wasn't losing sleep because he was working, he was losing sleep because he was anxious that he wasn't working. His hands and feet constantly felt cold. Doctors told him it was stress, though they couldn't be certain; his visits were all con-ducted via phone—there was no way he had time for an actual appoint-ment during normal business hours.

But he got the work done, and the model worked. It was effective and elegant. Insurance companies and hospitals all over the country used it. As a matter of fact, it worked so well that the White House called and asked if he would help them implement the law. He'd be a few reports away from the president. His friends who once joked he was "anti-fun" now joked that he might run the country one day. In this fast-paced world of high-stakes problem solving, he was a rising star. He was a few months shy of his 24th birthday.

BY NOW YOU MAY BE WONDERING: Who are these people, and how can I emulate their success? But that's not the story we're here to tell.

The high school running phenom never ran a step faster than he did that summer day at the Prefontaine Classic. And the young-gun consultant didn't go on to run for office or make partner at an esteemed firm. As a matter of fact, he left the White House and hasn't received a promotion since. Both runner and consultant shined extremely bright, only to see their performance plateau, their health suffer, and their satisfaction wane.

These stories aren't unique. They happen everywhere and can happen to anyone. Including us. We, the authors of this book, are the runner (Steve) and the consultant (Brad).

We met a couple years after we had both burnt out, and as we shared our stories over a few beers, we realized they were quite similar. At the time, we were both beginning our second lives: Steve as a performance scientist and budding coach of endurance athletes, and Brad as an emerging writer. Both of us were embarking on new journeys, and we couldn't help but wonder: Could we reach the highest levels of performance without repeating our previous failings?

What started out as a two-person support group morphed into a close friendship founded upon a shared interest in the science of performance. We became curious: Is healthy, sustainable peak performance possible? If so, how? What's the secret? What, if any, are the principles underlying great performance? How can people like us—which is to say, just about anyone—adopt them?

Consumed by these questions, we did what any scientist and journalist would do. We scoured the literature and spoke with countless great performers across various capabilities and domains—from mathematicians to scientists to artists to athletes—in search of answers. And like so many other reckless ideas conceived over a few glasses of alcohol, this book was born.

We can't guarantee that reading this book will set you on a

> *Is healthy, sustainable peak performance possible? If so, how? What's the secret? What, if any, are the principles underlying great performance? How can people like us—which is to say, just about anyone—adopt them?*

path to winning Olympic gold, painting the next masterpiece, or breaking ground in mathematical theory. Genetics play an unfortunately undeniable role in all of those things. What we can guarantee, however, is that reading this book will help you nurture your nature so that you can maximize your potential in a healthy and sustainable way.

INTRODUCTION
Great Expectations

Let's start with a simple question. Have you ever felt pressure to perform? If you answered no, perhaps you've hacked some meditative, Zen-like trance. Or maybe you just don't care much about, well, anything. In either case, this book probably isn't for you. But if you answered yes, then you can consider yourself to be like just about everyone else on the planet. So read on!

Whether in school, the office, the artist's studio, or the arena, at some point most of us have experienced a desire to take our game to the next level. And that's a good thing. The process of setting a goal on the outer boundaries of what we think is possible, and then systematically pursuing it, is one of the most fulfilling parts about being human. It's also a good thing that we want to take our game to the next level because, more than ever, we have no other choice.

The majority of this book is focused on showing you *how* to improve your performance. But first, let's set the stage by briefly exploring *why* doing so is more imperative than ever.

> *The process of setting a goal on the outer boundaries of what we think is possible, and then systematically pursuing it, is one of the most fulfilling parts about being human.*

UNPRECEDENTED PRESSURE

The bar for human performance is at an all-time high. New athletic records are being set weekly. College admissions requirements are at

The bar for human performance is at an all-time high.

unprecedented levels. Cutthroat competition is common in nearly every corner of the global economy. In his book *The Coming Jobs War*, Jim Clifton writes that we are on the precipice of "an all-out global war for good jobs." It would be one thing if a disgruntled employee was saying this on a ranting blog. Clifton, however, is anything but that. He is the chairman and CEO of Gallup, the global research firm that has an international reputation for its rigorous and scientific approach to polling. Clifton goes on to explain that recent polling at Gallup unequivocally shows that global competition has led to a shortage of "good jobs for good people." As a result, he writes, "An increasing number of people in the world are miserable, hopeless, suffering, and becoming dangerously unhappy."

Clifton paints a scary picture; unfortunately, he's right. Data shows the use of antidepressants by Americans has risen by 400 percent in the past decade and anxiety is at an all-time high. Though these conditions may have genetic roots, they are most likely also triggered by the environment we live in, the one that Clifton describes.

To grasp how we arrived at such an environment, we need look no further than the electronic devices we grasp most of the day. By placing the entire world within a few taps and swipes, digital technology opens up access to talent in a big way. Both the number of people available to do a given job and the places where a given job can be done have increased dramatically. Dan Schawbel, a human resource expert and author of the *New York Times* bestseller *Promote Yourself*, puts it this way: "This isn't the workplace of 10 years ago. There's a lot of pressure. And it's competitive in the sense that anyone in the world could take your job for less money, so you have to work harder." And in the workplace of 10 years from now, it won't just be other people we need to compete against but also a superhuman species that never tires and requires little self-care.

COMPETING AGAINST THE MACHINES

The use of computers, robots, and other sources of artificial intelligence is increasingly exerting pressure on human performance. This often happens in such subtle ways that we don't even notice. For example, by using ever more sophisticated technology to eliminate the need for physical space, inventory, and a salesforce, companies like Amazon can drive down their operating costs. This allows them to sell just about anything we might want at hugely discounted prices. But there is a dark side to such online megastores: the vast number of jobs they make obsolete. Indeed, the rise of Amazon marked the fall and eventual bankruptcy of some of their competition, notably the iconic brick-and-mortar bookstore Borders. At its peak, Borders employed about 35,000 people. That's a lot of lost jobs. The scariest part of this story is that, today, Amazon sells far more than books, and the company is starting to explore how it can deliver almost everything not with humans but with mechanical drones. Still happy with your Prime membership?

> The use of computers, robots, and other sources of artificial intelligence is increasingly exerting pressure on human performance.

It's not just retail and sales jobs that machines are crowding out. Zeynep Tufekci, PhD, a professor at the University of North Carolina who studies the social impacts of technology, writes, "The machines are getting smarter, and they're coming for more and more jobs." Over the past decade, machines have learned how to process regular spoken language, recognize human faces and read their expressions, classify personality types, and even carry out conversations.

Tufekci isn't alone in her concern about technology's escalating impact on humans. Some of the world's brightest minds agree. Physicist Stephen Hawking, serial inventor Elon Musk, Google's director of research Peter Norvig, and others cosigned an open letter calling for researchers to take special care in developing new artificial intelligence. Hawking told the BBC, "The primitive forms of artificial intelligence we already have proved very useful. But I think the development of full artificial intelligence could spell the end of the human race."

This book isn't about doomsday scenarios in which we find ourselves at war with machines. But in more ways than one, we are already waging that war. And in order to keep up with the machines, we will need to up our game. It's inevitable.

COMPETING AGAINST EACH OTHER

In 1954, when Sir Roger Bannister became the first ever person to run a mile in under 4 minutes, many thought it represented the outer limits of human performance. Shortly after crossing the tape, Bannister remarked, "Doctors and scientists said that breaking the 4-minute barrier was impossible, that one would die in the attempt. Thus, when I got up from the track after collapsing at the finish line, I figured I was dead."

Today, more than 20 Americans break the 4-minute barrier *every year*. When athletes in other countries, including running powerhouses such as Kenya and Ethiopia, are taken into account, experts speculate hundreds of people run sub-4 miles annually. Heck, some runners even do *training intervals* at this pace. Nuts is the new normal. Just look at the current mile record—3 minutes and 43 seconds—set by Hicham El Guerrouj in 1999. Sir Roger wouldn't even have been on the same straightaway when El Guerrouj was crossing the finish line.

In nearly all sports in which we compete against a clock, what were world records a half century ago are now regularly surpassed by high schoolers. Team sports, too, have become increasingly competitive over time. In 1947, the average height of a professional basketball player was about 6 feet 4 inches. Today, that number has grown to 6 feet 7 inches. It's not just genet-

In nearly all sports in which we compete against a clock, what were world records a half century ago are now regularly surpassed by high schoolers.

ically determined physical traits like height that have increased but also skills. If you watch game tape from the 1950s, you'll notice that even the point guards—the players who specialize in ball handling—dribbled almost exclusively with their dominant hand. Today, nearly every player on the court appears to be ambidextrous.

Why and how did this happen? Much like in the traditional economy, in the economy of sports the emergence of a global talent pool has increased the number of people "in the game" with ideal genetics for a specific sport as well as the number of people willing to dedicate themselves to achieving greatness. Layer on enhanced and more scientific training, nutrition, and recovery methods, and it becomes easier to comprehend the 16 seconds separating El Guerrouj and Bannister.*

INCREASED PRESSURE TO PERFORM is ubiquitous across domains. This is a movement with no end in sight, and if Stephen Hawking is right, we may only be experiencing the beginnings of it. It should come as no surprise, then, that people are going to great lengths in search of an edge.

GOING TO GREAT LENGTHS

Have you ever walked into a GNC, Vitamin Shoppe, or any other supplement vendor? If you have, and if you're anything like us, you've probably wondered: Who buys all these pills, powders, and shakes? Judging by the numbers, the answer is, well, just about everyone. Although only a tiny minority of the developed world's population has mineral or vitamin deficiencies that stand to benefit from supplementation, annual revenue in the global supplement industry regularly exceeds $100 billion.

Even more remarkable are the outlandish claims made by many of the

---

* We'd be remiss not to mention doping, or the illegal use of performance enhancing drugs. Unfortunately, doping has played an undeniable role in far too many record performances, something we explore in much more detail in this book. Still, the general uptick in performance across all of athletics is far too great to be attributed solely to doping.

manufacturers of top-selling supplements and related products. Take, for instance, a product called neuro Bliss—a drink that promises to reduce stress and enhance brain and body function. It sells for over $2 a bottle. While the company's website says, "In a fast-paced world, neuro drinks help to level the playing field," we've yet to see any science that backs up this claim. Yet neuro Bliss continues to be a popular-selling drink. People are desperate for an edge—any edge—even if there is no science to suggest that such an "edge" exists. Unfortunately, this kind of desperation is often the first step down a dangerous path into the world of exploiting controlled substances for performance enhancement.

IT WAS EXAM TIME at a major university and a student whom we'll call Sara couldn't help but notice a trend that was making her a bit more nervous than usual. More and more of her peers, students she'd be measured against, were taking Adderall. Intended to treat attention deficit hyperactivity disorder (ADHD), or the clinical inability to pay attention and focus, Adderall combines the stimulants levoamphetamine and dextroamphetamine, yielding what in essence is a tempered version of the street drug speed.

Although many experts believe the naturally occurring rate of ADHD is somewhere in the neighborhood of 5 to 6 percent of the population, data from the Centers for Disease Control and Prevention (CDC) show that the diagnosis is being made at twofold rates, or in about 11 percent of American youth. But from Sara's perspective, just about everyone on campus was using Adderall, regardless of whether they had an ADHD diagnosis or a prescription for the drug.

Why might this be the case? According to WebMD, which is a likely source for college students who are looking for a layman's description of a drug, Adderall "increases the ability to pay attention, concentrate, stay focused, and stop fidgeting." Never mind side effects that include loss of appetite, stomach pain, nausea, headache, insomnia, and hallucinations. These students, who had no sign of ADHD, were using Adderall like a steroid for the brain to get a psychological edge. This student drug abuse is much like athletes who abuse steroids in sports, where drugs initially intended to treat medical conditions are used illicitly by healthy individuals to gain a physical edge. Some researchers estimate that 30 percent of students turn to stimulants like Addcrall for nonmedical reasons. Not surprisingly, Adderall misuse is most common during periods of high stress, for instance during exams. Countless students report that the drug reduces fatigue while it increases reading comprehension, interest, cognition, and memory.

For a recent investigative report, CNN asked student-users about their experiences with Adderall. The answers sound like an infomercial:

- "The fact that it's illegal doesn't really cross my mind. It's not something that I get nervous about because it's so widespread and simple."

- "I just feel very alive and awake and ready for challenges that come my way."

- "I'm on page 15 of my paper in just a few hours . . . and I'm very confident in it."

No wonder Sara is feeling a bit under the gun. "I won't use [it] because I think it's cheating, but it's rampant—just rampant," she says.

IT'D BE BAD ENOUGH if the illicit use of drugs in search of an edge were confined to academic settings, but it seems this trend is becoming increasingly pervasive in the professional workplace as well. Kimberly Dennis, MD, is the medical director for a substance-abuse center outside of Chicago. She says she's observed a dramatic uptick in the use of drugs like Adderall in professionals ages 25 to 45, who, just like students, are looking to gain even the slightest advantage.

One such worker, Elizabeth, told the New York Times, "It is necessary— necessary for survival of the best and smartest and highest-achieving people." During the process of founding an innovative health technology company, Elizabeth sensed that working hard simply wasn't enough. She felt she had to put in more time, and sleep was getting in the way. So she turned to Adderall. "Friends of mine, people in finance and on Wall Street, are traders and had to start at five in the morning and be on top of their games—most of them were taking Adderall. You can't be the sluggish one . . . it's like this at most companies I know with driven young people— there's a certain expectation of performance."

Anjan Chatterjee, MD, chief of neurology at Pennsylvania Hospital and author of *The Aesthetic Brain*, sees the use of workplace productivity drugs as the "probable future." Americans will continue to work longer hours and take fewer vacations. "Why not add drugs to energize, focus, and limit that annoying waste of time—sleep?"

Though it may seem like a dire one, Chatterjee's prediction is not unique. Another expert who agrees with him is Erik Parens, a behavioral scientist at the ethics think tank The Hastings Center. He says that the epidemic of stimulant use in America is simply a symptom of modern life: on your game 24/7, tethered to your email, needing to perform better today than you did yesterday. But that doesn't mean this lifestyle, nor the stimulant use required to support it, is a good thing. As we'll soon learn, drugs or no drugs, performing in this non-stop manner without sufficient rest is suboptimal at best and dangerous at worse. A culture that pushes people to break the law and cheat just to stay in the game, let alone get ahead, is not a good one—nor is it sustainable.

A culture that pushes people to break the law and cheat just to stay in the game, let alone get ahead, is not a good one.

When Chatterjee and other experts talk about workplace doping, they often draw analogies to sports—intensely competitive, high-stakes, win-at-all-costs environments where even the most marginal advantage can produce huge gains. Unfortunately, if the workplace is truly moving in the same direction as sports, that's very bad news for everyone.

BIGGER, FASTER, STRONGER—
BUT AT WHAT COST?

Home run records, Tour de France yellow jerseys, and Olympic medals represent feats of superhuman performance. Unfortunately, many of these performances have proven to be just that: superhuman. They are illusions aided by pharmacological resources and medical sophistication that rivals what you'd find at the best hospitals. Although less than 2 percent of dopers are caught, research suggests that up to 40 percent of elite athletes use banned substances to enhance their performance. More than a quarter of the athletes we watch on TV could be competing dirty.

While it's easy to think the problem is limited to the upper echelons of sport, that couldn't be further from the truth. Doping is alive and well in collegiate, high school, and amateur athletics. A 2013 survey conducted by the Partnership for Drug-Free Kids showed that 11 percent of high schoolers used synthetic human growth hormone (HGH) at least once in the prior year. Let that sink in. Eleven percent of teenagers are injecting a chemical rendition of the body's most powerful hormone straight into their developing bodies. Perhaps the only thing more disconcerting is that these high schoolers might be drawing inspiration from their parents.

It's unfortunate but true. Competitive weekend warriors—middle-age amateur men and women trying to win their age group in running, cycling, and triathlon races—have increasingly been caught using performance enhancing drugs. The problem is so large that the governing bodies of these sports are implementing drug testing programs even for those who aren't racing for a paycheck. David Epstein, a well-respected investigative reporter who covers doping, dug deep into the world of performance enhancing drug (PED) use among weekend warriors. What he found isn't pretty: He says that some $120 billion are attributed to "anti-aging," much of which is the peddling of steroids to middle-age men. This market is only destined to grow as baby boomers, with their disposable incomes and desire to stay young and competitive, grow older. Epstein sums up the situation in the report's title: "Everyone's Juicing."

THE CONSEQUENCES OF THIS performance-at-any-cost culture cannot be overstated. Unbelievable performances, the type that once lifted individuals to stardom, are now literally unbelievable. Whenever anyone does something great, be it on campus, at the workplace, or on the playing field, we are forced to question their integrity. As Michael Joyner, MD, an expert on human performance at the Mayo Clinic, says, "We live in a world where all exceptional performances are suspect." However sad this state of affairs may be on a cultural level, it's perhaps even worse on an individual one. This is especially the case for those who, like the student Sara, choose to compete clean and not to sacrifice their health and morality. As a result, people like Sara are forced to raise their game to an illusory bar. Far too often, the outcome is a bad one.

Unbelievable performances, the type that once lifted individuals to stardom, are now literally unbelievable.

BURNOUT

A 2014 survey of over 2,500 companies in 90 countries worldwide found that a pressing challenge for most modern employers is "the overwhelmed employee." Workers, perhaps fearful that they must always be "on" because someone else will be, check their cell phones almost 150 times per day. And when they swipe to the right on their devices, what they find is an utterly overwhelming amount of information. One study found that more than half of white-collar workers believe they've reached a breaking point: They simply can't handle any more information, and they report feeling demoralized as a result.

Even so, regardless of how futile our efforts might be, we feel compelled to keep up. This urge is especially common among Americans. Only a third of American workers say they take a proper lunch break (i.e., leave their desks). The other 66 percent opt to eat while working, or not at all. It's not just lunch that Americans are working through, but dinner, nights, and weekends, too. In an aptly titled paper, "Americans Work Too

Long (And Too Often at Strange Times)," economists Daniel Hamermesh and Elena Stancanelli found that 27 percent of Americans regularly work between 10 p.m. and 6 a.m., and 29 percent of Americans do at least some work on the weekends.

It would be one thing if we were making up for our workaholic tendencies by taking elongated breaks to recharge and rejuvenate. But that's not the case. On average, American workers leave 5 vacation days unused at the end of each and every year. When you add all of this up, as Gallup did in 2014, you find that the typical American workweek is 47 hours, not 40. In other words, American workers are grinding away for almost an entire extra day each

American workers are grinding away for almost an entire extra day each and every week.

and every week. Against this backdrop, it's by no means shocking that 53 percent of American workers report feeling burnt out.

Nonstop, frenetic work won't just leave us feeling completely depleted; it's also bad for our health. One extreme case is that of 21-year-old Moritz Erhardt, an intern at Bank of America Merrill Lynch who, after working 72 hours straight, was found dead in his shower. According to an autopsy, he died of an epileptic seizure that might have been triggered by fatigue. Shortly after Erhardt's tragic death, Goldman Sachs, another preeminent investment house, put a restriction on the number of hours interns could work in a day: 17.

Less extreme than Erhardt's awful story, but far more common, are cases where unsustainable workloads and constant tension contribute to anxiety, depression, insomnia, obesity, infertility, blood disorders, cardiovascular disease, and a host of other biophysical consequences that are detrimental to both our quality and quantity of life. The irony is that burnout isn't just common in the corporate world but also in fields that exist to educate people on health and to help them achieve it. Studies have found that over 57 percent of medical residents and up to 46 percent of bona fide physicians meet the criteria for burnout. Other research shows that over 30 percent of teachers suffer from burnout as well.

THE SEEMINGLY IMPRISONED 9-TO-5 worker might envy the flexibility and freedom of an artist or writer, but it turns out flexibility and freedom are not the cure-alls to burnout that we imagine them to be. Nearly every artist has struggled with creative burnout at some point in their career. Burnout is common in artists because their passion serves as both a gift and a curse. A gift, because, as Plato remarked in the 4th century BCE, passion is "the channel by which we receive the greatest blessings," fueling original, imaginative, and inspired work. But left unchecked, passion can drive artists to work themselves into the ground.

Obsession, perfectionism, hypersensitivity, the need for control, and high expectations are common traits in great artists, and they are all linked to creative burnout. Add to this the pressure of making a living as an artist, harsh criticisms, social comparison, and the solitary nature of creative work, and it becomes easier to understand why so many artists suffer from burnout, or worse. Research shows that people who work in creative fields are especially susceptible to anxiety, depression, alcoholism, and suicide.

Another pursuit in which passion and pressure commonly collide is athletics, where burnout is one of the main reasons why everyone—from kids to weekend warriors to professional athletes—quits playing sports. So frequently do athletes push themselves too hard without taking a break that there is even a medical term for it: overtraining syndrome. In overtraining syndrome, the central nervous system is thrown out of whack, yielding a cascade of negative biological effects. Ultimately, overtraining syndrome results in deep fatigue, illness, injury, and performance decline. It's the body's way of saying "I'm done—absolutely no more." A forced shutdown of sorts.

Overtraining syndrome sounds like something to avoid at all costs, especially if you make a living with your body. Yet over 60 percent of elite runners say they've been overtrained at some point in their careers. Somewhat surprisingly, it's not just elite athletes who succumb to the temptation to do more when their bodies are tell-

Thirty to 40 percent of high school and amateur athletes have suffered from overtraining at least once in their sporting careers.

ing them to do less: Thirty to 40 percent of high school and amateur athletes have suffered from overtraining at least once in their sporting careers.

BY NOW IT SHOULD BE CLEAR that pressure to perform comes from all directions. As a result, more and more people are working themselves beyond the point of diminishing returns. Some are even turning to performance enhancing drugs, risking their health and reputation while breaking ethical and legal codes. Is this really the new requirement for success in today's society? There's got to be a better way.

It turns out, there is. The rest of this book is dedicated to exploring it.

A BETTER WAY

Over the past few years, we've had the privilege of delving deep into the practices of top performers across a wide range of capabilities and domains. We've studied, interviewed, observed, and in some cases worked with individuals who are not only at the top of their game, but who are also at the top of *the* game. In doing so, we couldn't help but notice striking similarities in how these great performers approach their work. It turns out that whether someone is trying to qualify for the Olympics, break ground in mathematical theory, or craft an artistic masterpiece, many of the principles underlying healthy, sustainable success are the same.

> *It turns out that whether someone is trying to qualify for the Olympics, break ground in mathematical theory, or craft an artistic masterpiece, many of the principles underlying healthy, sustainable success are the same.*

These principles—each time-tested, safe, ethical, and legal—have been used by great performers for centuries. Only now, however, is fascinating new science revealing why and how these performance principles work. This understanding makes them accessible to everyone. The rest of this book is dedicated to examining these principles inside and out, merging story with science to leave you, the reader, with concrete, evidence-based, and practical takeaways to help you improve your game.

Our journey into understanding the science and art of performance requires us to make links between traditionally siloed domains. It is through these overlooked connections that powerful performance insights emerge. In the words of Eric Weiner, author and innovation expert, breakthroughs occur when "people realize the arbitrary nature of their own [field] and open their minds to, in effect, the possibility of possibility. Once you realize there is another way of doing X, or thinking about Y, then all sorts of new channels open up to you." With that in mind, throughout this book we'll uncover what an artist can learn from an athlete, what an intellectual can learn from an artist, and what an athlete can learn from an intellectual.

We'll show you how strengthening your ability to solve complex cognitive problems is similar to strengthening your ability to lift weights—that the world's best thinkers and the world's best powerlifters follow the same processes to elicit growth. We'll investigate the influence of routine and environment, and explain how and why the pregame warmups of all-star athletes, artists, and public speakers are so alike and so effective. We'll even discuss fashion, and use science to explain why the geniuses of yesterday, such as Albert Einstein, and the geniuses of today, such as Mark Zuckerberg, don't care much about it. We'll explore why after they achieve breakthroughs—be it painting a masterpiece, penning an award-winning novel, or setting a world record in sport—so many great performers often thank and attribute their success to forces beyond themselves: be it family, God, or some other transcendent power.

If we've done our job well, by the time you finish reading this book, you'll thoroughly understand:

- The scientific cycle behind growth and development
- How to prime for peak performance and daily productivity
- The power of purpose as a performance enhancer

Far more important, though, you'll be able to use these concepts in your own pursuits, whatever those pursuits may be. To help you in doing so, throughout the book you'll find brief sections titled "Performance Practices." These sections are meant to hammer home key points and help you reflect on how you can apply them to your own life.

THE GROWTH EQUATION

1

THE SECRET TO SUSTAINABLE SUCCESS

Think for a moment about what it takes to make muscles, such as your biceps, stronger. If you try lifting weights that are too heavy, you probably won't make it past one repetition. And even if you do, you're liable to hurt yourself along the way. Lift too light a weight, on the other hand, and you won't see much, if any, result; your biceps simply won't grow. You've got to find the Goldilocks weight: an amount you can barely manage, that will leave you exhausted and fatigued—but not injured—by the time you've finished your workout. Yet discovering such an ideal weight is only half the battle.

> *Stress + rest = growth. This equation holds true regardless of what you are trying to grow.*

If you lift every day, multiple times a day, without much rest in between, you're almost certainly going to burn out.

But if you hardly ever make it to the gym and fail to regularly push your limits, you're not going to get much stronger, either. The key to strengthening your biceps—and, as we'll learn, any muscle, be it physical, cognitive, or emotional—is balancing the right amount of stress with the right amount of rest. Stress + rest = growth. This equation holds true regardless of what it is that you are trying to grow.

PERIODIZATION

In the world of exercise science, this cycle of stress and rest is often referred to as periodization. Stress—and by this we don't mean fighting with your partner or your boss, but rather, some sort of stimulus, such as lifting a heavy weight—challenges the body, in some cases pushing it close to failure. This process is usually followed by a slight dip in function; just think about how useless your arms are after a hard weight-lifting session. But if after the stressful period you give your body time to rest and recover, it adapts and becomes stronger, allowing you to push a little harder in the future. Over time, the cycle looks like this:

1. Isolate the muscle or capability you want to grow

2. Stress it

3. Rest and recover, allowing for adaptation to occur

4. Repeat—this time stressing the muscle or capability a bit more than you did the last time

World-class athletes are masters at this cycle. On a micro level, their training alternates between hard days (e.g., intervals until the brink of muscle failure and total exhaustion) and easy days (e.g., jogging at a pedestrian pace). The best athletes also prioritize recovery, time on the couch and in bed, just as much as they prioritize time on the track or in the gym. On a more macro level, great athletes often follow a hard month of training with an easy week. They intentionally design their seasons to include only a few peak events that are followed by periods of physical and psychological restoration. The days, weeks, months, years, and entire careers of master athletes represent a continual ebb and flow between stress and rest. Those who can't figure out the right balance either get hurt or burn out (too much stress, not enough rest) or become complacent and plateau (not enough stress, too much rest). Those who can figure out the right balance, however, become life-long champions.

SUSTAINABLE PERFORMANCE

When Deena Kastor graduated from the University of Arkansas in 1996, she was a good collegiate runner who had never quite pulled off a major victory. She received multiple All-American awards and stood atop many podiums, but the collegiate national championship was always just a touch—a few seconds, to be precise—out of reach. This didn't deter Kastor from going all-in on running. Upon graduation, she connected with the legendary coach Joe Vigil and followed him to the oxygen-deprived air of Alamosa, Colorado, and ultimately to Mammoth Lakes, California. There, training at 9,000 feet above sea level, Kastor went to work on reaching a level far beyond what her collegiate success could have predicted.

Glimpse into Kastor's training diary during her prime and one word comes to mind: extraordinary. A 24-mile-long run at 7,000 feet altitude; mile repeats at speeds that for most people would be equivalent to an all-out 100-yard dash; and her favorite, 4 by 2 miles at a lung-searing 5-minute-mile pace, all on the highest path in Mammoth Lakes. These heroic workouts make up only a small portion of Kastor's total running. At the end of each week, in the bottom right corner of her training journal, she circled "total miles run." This number almost always read between 110 and 140. While this may seem extraordinary, to Kastor it was all very ordinary. As a result, she reached the highest levels of athletic success.

Deena Kastor is hands-down the name most associated with American women's running, and for good reason. She's won an Olympic bronze medal in the marathon, and has earned distinction in many major national races. She holds the American marathon record, having covered the 26.2 miles in just 2 hours and 19 minutes, or at a pace of 5 minutes and 20 seconds per mile. Just think about running one mile that fast, and then imagine doing it 26 times in a row. Perhaps even harder to comprehend is the 2 hour and 27 minute marathon (5 minute and 40 second mile pace) she ran at age 42. That's right, Kastor is still running insanely fast well into what should be the twilight of her endurance sports career. And although she may lose an occasional race to someone 10 to 20 years her junior, she's consistently at the front of the pack, racing against, and often beating, women young enough to be her daughters.

Ask Kastor how she's been able to sustain this level of performance and you'll get a lesson in periodization. While Kastor's quick to mention the hard work she puts in, she's equally as quick to mention the rest that follows. "The leaps and bounds I've made over the last several years have come from outside the training environment and how I choose to recover," she told *Competitor* magazine in 2009. "During a workout you're breaking down soft tissue and really stressing your body. How you treat yourself in between workouts is where you make gains and acquire the strength to attack the next one."

Kastor says she realized early on that simply working hard wouldn't do. She's even called her workouts the easy part. What sets her apart, the magic that has allowed her to run so fast and so far for the past 25 years, is how she recovers: the 10 to 12 hours of sleep she gets each night; her meticulous approach to diet; her weekly massage and stretching sessions. In other words, it's all the things she does when she isn't training that allows her to do what she does when she is. Stress demands rest, and rest supports stress. Kastor has mastered the inputs, and understands how much stress she can tolerate and how much rest she requires. Thus, the output—a lifetime of growth and excellence—isn't all that surprising.

Stress demands rest, and rest supports stress.

ALL THE BEST FOLLOW STRESS AND REST

Kastor is certainly unique, but her story is echoed by the research of Stephen Seiler. In 1996, shortly after earning his PhD in physiology in the United States, Seiler relocated to Norway. When he first arrived, he noticed something that befuddled him: During cross-training runs, world-class cross-country skiers were stopping before hills and then slowly *walking* up. Seiler didn't understand. Why were some of the best endurance athletes on the planet training so easily?

Seiler tracked down Norway's national cross-country ski coach, Inge Bråten, the man behind the training of legends such as eight-time Gold medalist Bjørn Dæhlie. He asked Bråten if he was imagining athletes slowly walking up hills in their training, and if not, could Bråten please explain what was going on. Bråten simply told Seiler that the skiers he saw walking had recently trained hard, so now they must train easy.

Upon hearing this, Seiler's mind flashed back to a paper he'd read that claimed Kenyan runners spent a majority of their training time running at a snail's pace. When he revisited the research, Seiler also saw it mentioned that the Kenyans alternated between very hard days and very easy days. At that moment, it struck Seiler that the best summer athletes in the world and the best winter athletes in the world appeared to be training quite similarly. As any good scientist would, he set out to test his hypothesis.

Seiler tracked the training of elite athletes across a variety of endurance sports including running, skiing, swimming, and cycling. He found that, irrespective of sport or nationality, their training followed roughly the same distribution. The best athletes in the world weren't adhering to a "no pain, no gain" model, nor were they doing fitness-magazine popularized high-intensity interval training (HIIT) or random "workouts of the day." Rather, they were systematically alternating between bouts of very intense work and periods of easy training and recovery, even if that meant *walking* up hills. The ongoing progression and development of elite competitors, Seiler found, was an exercise in stress and rest.

INTELLECTUAL AND CREATIVE DEVELOPMENT

Around the same time that Seiler was exploring commonalities among the top endurance athletes in the world, another researcher was exploring commonalities among the top creative and intellectual performers in the world. This researcher was Mihaly Csikszentmihalyi (pronounced chick-sent-mi-hi), PhD, a pioneer in the field of positive psychology known for his ideas on happiness, meaning, and optimal performance. If you've ever heard of the term "flow"—or a state of being fully absorbed in an activity with laserlike focus, completely in the zone—that's Csikszentmihalyi's work.

Less known than his work on flow, but equally insightful, is Csikszentmihalyi's study of creativity. Over the course of 50 years, he conducted hundreds of interviews with field-altering geniuses from diverse domains. He spoke with groundbreaking inventors, innovative artists, Nobel Prize–winning scientists, and Pulitzer Prize–winning writers. Just as Seiler found that world-class endurance athletes migrate toward a similar style of work, Csikszentmihalyi found that the same held true for creative geniuses: the brightest minds spend their time either pursuing an activity with ferocious intensity, or engaging in complete restoration and recovery. This approach, Csikszentmihalyi discovered, not only prevents creative burnout and cognitive fatigue, but it also fosters breakthrough ideas and discoveries (we'll explore why this happens in more detail in Chapter 4). Csikszentmihalyi documented a common process across almost all great intellectual and creative performers, regardless of their field:

The brightest minds spend their time either pursuing their activity with ferocious intensity, or engaging in complete restoration and recovery.

1. Immersion: total engagement in their work with deep, unremitting focus

---

PERFORMANCE PRACTICES

- Alternate between cycles of stress and rest in your most important pursuits.
- Insert short breaks throughout your work over the course of a day.
- Strategically time your "off-days," long weekends, and vacations to follow periods of heavy stress.
- Determine when your work regularly starts to suffer. When you find that point, insert a recovery break just prior to it.

---

2. Incubation: a period of rest and recovery when they are not at all thinking about their work

3. Insight: the occurrence of "aha" or "eureka" moments—the emergence of new ideas and growth in their thinking

Look familiar? The manner in which great intellectual and creative performers continually grow their minds mirrors the manner in which great physical performers continually grow their bodies. Perhaps this is because our muscles and minds are more alike than we might think. Just as our muscles deplete and run out of energy, as we're about to see, our minds do, too.

MIND AS A MUSCLE

In the mid-1990s, Roy Baumeister, PhD, a social psychologist who at the time was teaching at Case Western Reserve University, revolutionized how we think about the mind and its capacity. Baumeister wanted to get to the bottom of common-day struggles such as why we feel mentally "tired" after toiling away at a complex problem. Or when we are on a diet, why we are more likely to crack at night after diligently resisting unhealthy food all day. In other words, Baumeister was interested in understanding how and why our intellectual power and our willpower run out of gas.

When Baumeister set out to solve this problem, he didn't need the latest and greatest brain-imaging technology. All he needed were some cookies and radishes.

In an elegantly designed experiment, Baumeister and his colleagues had 67 adults file into a room that smelled like chocolate chip cookies. After the participants had taken their seats, freshly baked cookies were brought into the room. No sooner than everyone's salivary glands began working, things got interesting. While half the study participants were allowed to eat the cookies, the other half were prohibited from doing so. Adding insult to injury, the non-cookie-eaters were given radishes and told they could eat them instead.

As you might imagine, the cookie-eaters had no problem with the first part of the experiment. Like most people in their situation, they enjoyed indulging. The radish-eaters, on the other hand, struggled mightily. "The [radish-eaters] exhibited clear interest in the cookies, to the point of looking lovingly at the display and in a few cases even picking up the cookies to sniff them," writes Baumeister. Resisting the cookies was no easy task.

This doesn't seem groundbreaking. Who wouldn't struggle to resist delicious desserts? But things got even more interesting in the second part of the experiment, during which the radish-eaters' struggles continued. After both groups finished eating, all participants were asked to solve a seemingly solvable, but actually unsolvable, problem. (Yes, this was a cruel experiment, especially for those stuck with the radishes.) The radish-eaters lasted a little over 8 minutes and gave the problem 19 attempts. The cookie-eaters, on the other hand, persisted for over 20 minutes and attempted to solve the problem 33 times. Why the stark difference? Because the radish-eaters had depleted their mental muscle by resisting the cookies, whereas the cookie-eaters had a full tank of psychological gas and thus exerted far more effort in trying to solve the problem.

Baumeister went on to repeat several variations of this study, and he observed the same result every time. Participants who were forced to flex their mental muscle—be it to resist temptation, solve a hard puzzle, or make tough decisions—performed worse on a subsequent task that also required mental energy as compared to participants in a control group who had an easy first task, like eating fresh cookies.

RESISTING COOKIES IS A DANGEROUS GAME

It seems we have a single reservoir of brainpower for all acts of cognition and self-control, even those that are unrelated. When people are asked to suppress their emotions when under duress—for example, not showing frustration or sadness while watching a tragic film—they subsequently struggle on a wide range of unrelated tasks, such as resisting tempting foods or storing items in working memory. The phenomenon doesn't stop there. Even physical challenges (e.g., performing a

> We have a single reservoir of brainpower for all acts of cognition and self-control, even those that are unrelated.

wall sit) can be impaired by exerting your mental muscle beforehand. Research shows that even if their bodies are fresh, the physical performance of people who are mentally fatigued suffers. Put differently, the boundaries between mental and physical fatigue are not nearly as defined as we think.

In a study cleverly titled "Hungry for Love: The Influence of Self-Regulation on Infidelity," 32 college students in exclusive relationships interacted via chat room with a confederate (i.e., a researcher playing along) of the opposite sex. Prior to this chat, half the study participants were forced to resist eating a tempting food, while the other half could eat to their hearts' desire. As you might expect, those who were forced to resist the tempting food were more likely to give their phone number to, and even accept a coffee date with, the confederate. The study authors concluded, "Weakened self-control may be one potential cause for the levels of infidelity occurring in romantic relationships today." You may want to think twice before encouraging your significant other to go on a diet. (But you probably already knew that.)

A LOOK INSIDE YOUR TIRED BRAIN

More recently, researchers have started studying the notion of a mental muscle with fancy imaging technology instead of just cookies and radishes. What they are finding is quite intriguing. They put people with depleted mental muscles in an fMRI machine (a technology that lets researchers look at activity inside the brain) and discovered the brain of a tired person acts in a peculiar way. When shown a tempting image, such as a juicy cheeseburger, or asked to solve a hard problem, activity in parts of the brain associated with emotional response (the amygdala and orbitofrontal cortex) supersede activity in the part of the brain tasked with thoughtful, rational thinking (the prefrontal cortex). Other experiments show that after someone is forced to exert self-control, activity in the prefrontal cortex diminishes altogether. It's no wonder that when we are mentally drained we struggle with complex problems and self-control, opting for cartoons and cookies instead.

Much like how after you've lifted weights to the point of fatigue your arms won't function very well, after you've used your mind to the point of

---

PERFORMANCE PRACTICES

- Remember that "stress is stress": fatigue on one task spills over into the next, even if the two are completely unrelated.

- Only take on a few challenges at once. Otherwise you'll literally run out of energy.

- Tweak your environment to support your goals. This is especially important at times when you know you'll be depleted. It's incredible how much our surroundings impact our behavior, especially when we are fatigued.

fatigue—be it to resist temptation, make tough decisions, or work on challenging cognitive tasks—it, too, won't function very well. This fatigue might lead you to eat cookies, give up on solving a tough intellectual problem, or even prematurely give in during physical challenges. In the worst case, you might even cheat on your significant other.

The good news is that just like the body, by stressing and allowing the mind to recover it also becomes stronger. Scientists have discovered that the more we resist temptation, think deeply, or focus intensely, the better we become at doing so. A new line of research contests that willpower in particular is not as limited as scientists once thought, and suggests that by successfully completing smaller productive changes we can build the strength to complete larger ones in the future. Either way, whether it is the result of willpower, ego-depletion, or some other mechanism, we cannot continuously use our mind (at least not effectively) without at some point experiencing fatigue. And we cannot take on more sizeable psychological challenges without first building strength through smaller ones. All of this takes us back to where we started: stress + rest = growth.

THE RHYTHM OF STRESS AND REST

Over the next four chapters, we'll explore each component (stress and rest) of the growth equation in great detail. You'll learn the best ways to stress and rest both your physical and psychological muscles so that you can optimize your performance over the course of a day, month, year, and lifetime. But before we go there, to reinforce the universal truth about the power of cycling between stress and rest, we'll leave you with the remarkable story of someone who harnessed it to achieve excellence with *both* his mind and his body.

Josh Waitzkin first discovered chess in New York City's Washington Square Park when he was 6 years old. He set out to the park intent on playing on the monkey bars but when he arrived, Waitzkin was captivated by the fast-paced games of chess being played by adults across the way. The checkered board and the pieces that moved across it were a miniature world that Waitzkin would soon throw himself into and, eventually, master.

Waitzkin's mastery of chess didn't happen overnight, but close to it. While at first the young kid was nothing more than a novelty to the much-older regulars, it wasn't long before he was beating them. By age 8, Waitzkin was a dominant force, regularly defeating players five times his age. Anyone who bore witness to the Josh Waitzkin show couldn't help but notice his talent and passion for the game. Word spread quickly and it wasn't long before some of the world's finest chess masters were lining up to coach and mentor him.

From age 9 onward, Waitzkin took the US junior chess scene by storm, winning multiple national championships. At age 13, he became a National Master, one of the youngest ever chess players to earn the prestigious title. By the time he turned 16, Waitzkin had become an International Master. That same year, he was crowned US junior co-champion, an especially impressive feat given the division includes players up to age 21. The following year, he won the same championship outright.

Around the same time, Paramount Pictures released the hit film *Searching for Bobby Fischer*, which chronicled Waitzkin's rise to the top of chess. The movie illuminated what happens when deep talent meets deep passion and hard, smart work. It's a good thing Waitzkin wasn't *so* intent on the monkey bars in Washington Square Park, otherwise he might never have become an international superstar for his achievements in chess.

Just a few years later, however, when he was in his early 20s, like so many other young adults, Waitzkin's interests shifted. He became absorbed in meditation and Eastern philosophy. These new interests eventually led him to the Chinese martial art tai chi. Although he was drawn to the sport and immersed himself in it for its own sake, he was also happy to be out of the spotlight that accompanied his stardom in chess. That reprieve wouldn't last long.

Much like in chess, it wasn't long before Waitzkin had ascended to the top of the martial arts world. For the second time in his life, word spread quickly about the young man with great talent and passion. He drew interest and eventual coaching and mentorship from the best tai chi teachers in the world. He won numerous national championships in just his first few years in the sport. Before he had reached 30, Waitzkin was a world champion in fixed step push hands and moving step push hands, the primary competitive iterations of tai chi.

No doubt about it, Waitzkin has natural talent; we'd be foolish to discount the role of genetics in his accomplishments. But it's hard to believe that he simply has the best DNA for *everything*. As he laid out in his wonderful book, *The Art of Learning*, it's how he cultivated that talent and his competitive drive—how he nurtured his nature—that propelled him to the top of seemingly disparate domains. Waitzkin attributes much of his success in both chess and tai chi to alternating between stress and rest:

> *There was more than one occasion that I got up from the board four or five hours into a hugely tense chess game, walked outside the playing hall and sprinted fifty yards or up six flights of stairs. Then I'd walk back, wash my face, and be completely renewed. To this day, virtually every element of my physical training also revolves around one form or another of stress and recovery . . . If you are interested in really improving as a performer, I would suggest incorporating the rhythm of stress and recovery into all aspects of your life.*

RETHINKING
STRESS

n 1934, in McGill University's biochemistry department, a 28-year-old endocrinologist and assistant professor of medicine was attempting to discover a new hormone. His name was Hans Selye and he had every reason to believe he was making progress. When he injected rats with ovarian extract, hoping to elicit changes that could only be explained by an undiscovered sex hormone, the rats experienced a unique physiological response. Their adrenal cortexes became enlarged and their immune systems were activated. The more extract he injected, the greater the response. Selye was certain that a new sex hormone was triggering these physiological changes. He was elated. "At the age of 28, I already seemed to be on the track of a new hormone," he wrote in his journal.

Unfortunately for Selye, his enthusiasm wilted when he observed the same response after injecting rats with completely different fluids that had nothing to do with the reproductive system. Even a simple saline solution triggered the same response. His elation turned into heartbreak: "All my dreams of discovering a new hormone were shattered. All of the time and all the materials that went into this long study were wasted. I became so depressed that for a few days I could not do any work at all. I just sat in the laboratory, brooding." Though he didn't know it at the time, Selye's insistent brooding would turn out to be a blessing in disguise.

As Selye continued to ruminate upon his experiments, eventually it occurred to him that perhaps he should evaluate what he had witnessed from a different angle entirely: Maybe the liquid in the injection wasn't causing the response. Maybe the cause was the trauma of the injection itself. With that thought in mind, Selye emerged quickly from his rut and went about systematically traumatizing rats. He injected them, shocked them, operated on them, and everything in between. With each new act of trauma, he observed the same response: The rats' adrenal and immune systems became active. The rats weren't readying themselves for sex. They were readying themselves for a fight.

While Selye's dreams of discovering a new hormone were dashed, his consolation prize was a big one. He unknowingly stumbled upon a concept that would become one of the foremost concerns in modern society: stress. By doing something—anything, really—that shocked or caused pain and discomfort in the rats, he could trigger an innate stress response that we now know is shared by just about every living organism.

THE DOSE MAKES THE POISON

Selye and those who would build upon his work started stressing humans and observed the same phenomenon that they saw in rats. But they also noticed something else. Over time, humans and rats alike seemed to adapt to each unique stressor, building up increased resistance. Certain stressors could even produce desirable effects, strengthening the specific part of the body that was under duress. They learned that stress isn't just harmful; it can also serve as a stimulus for growth and adaptation.

We now know our adaptive stress response is rooted in molecules called inflammatory proteins and a hormone called cortisol. Inflammatory proteins and cortisol are activated by stress and serve as biological messengers, telling the

Stress isn't just harmful; it can also serve as a stimulus for growth and adaptation.

body, "We're not strong enough to withstand this attack!" As a result, the body marshals an army of biochemical building blocks and directs them to the area under stress, making the body stronger and more resilient. This is the body's incredible, preprogrammed way of better preparing itself to face future threats.

As we mentioned earlier, strengthening a muscle, such as your bicep, is a wonderful example of how stress works in a positive way. Lifting a heavy weight to the point of exhaustion causes micro-tears in the muscle's tissue and triggers the stress response. The body becomes aware that it's currently not strong enough to tolerate the stress it is under. Consequently, once we cease lifting weights, the body transitions into something called an anabolic state, in which the muscle is built up so it can withstand more stress in the future. This same process unfolds after just about any hard physical effort—from lifting weights to running to rowing to a challenging CrossFit workout.

If the amount of stress is too large or lasts too long, however, the body fails to adapt. It actually does the opposite of growing stronger: it deteriorates. Selye called this the "exhaustion stage." Today, many refer to the exhaustion stage as being under "chronic stress." The body rebels and enters something called a catabolic process, or a state of persistent breakdown. Rather than signaling for repair and then subsiding, elevated inflammation and cortisol linger at toxic levels. The adrenal system, constantly on guard, becomes overworked and fatigued. This is why it's not at all surprising that chronic stress contributes to myriad health problems; the body as a whole can withstand only so much tension before it breaks.

Put all this together, and a paradox emerges. Stress can be positive, triggering desirable adaptations in the body; or stress can be negative,

The effects of stress depend almost entirely on the dose.

causing grave damage and harm. The effects of stress depend almost entirely on the dose. And when applied in the right dose, stress does more than stimulate physiological adaptations. It stimulates psychological ones, too.

SKILLS COME FROM STRUGGLE

In reflecting upon his development as an elite performer, Josh Waitzkin, the international chess prodigy turned martial arts world champion who was profiled at the end of Chapter 1, had an interesting insight: Growth comes at the point of resistance; we learn by pushing ourselves to the outer reaches of our abilities.

Although it sounds like Waitzkin is referring to a grueling martial arts workout, that's not the case. Waitzkin is referring to his process for mastering chess. Well before he even knew what tai chi was, during his chess practices Waitzkin was stressing *his mind* to the point of complete exhaustion. While there are countless books about applying athletic training to nonathletic pursuits, Waitzkin did the opposite. He took the training philosophy that turned him into a world champion in chess and used it to become a world champion in martial arts. Even when he was training only his mind, meticulously studying chess patterns and the deep structure underlying them, Waitzkin had to stress himself. In order to elicit growth, he had to push at the point of resistance. Although Waitzkin's insight occurred over 20 years ago, the latest science on learning is beginning to uncover why his method works.

THE FRUSTRATIONS OF TEACHERS at a public high school in Oakland County, Michigan, are similar to those of teachers all over the country: oversized classes; digital device distractions; and, of course, not enough resources. But more than anything, the teachers are frustrated with the "Common Core," a standardized national curriculum to which they have been required to adhere. However well-intentioned the Common Core may be (it aims to ensure a national baseline of education at each grade level), its result in Oakland County has not been a good one. On a recent visit, we heard the following:*

- "I get where [the federal government] is coming from in wanting some standards in education, but the result is a cookie-cutter approach to teaching. It forces us to teach to the curriculum instead of teaching to the students." (Eleventh-grade science teacher)

- "It zaps the creativity right out of the classroom because it forces us to teach to certain tests." (Ninth-grade English teacher)

- "It's awful. It forces us to spoon-feed students. It's especially bad for the brightest kids since we don't have the freedom to push them. All the teaching happens inside a box." (Tenth-grade economics teacher)

These complaints have merit. Drilling specific, testable facts in preparation for rigid, standardized tests doesn't promote learning. Rather, science shows that learning demands open-ended exploration that allows students to reach beyond their individual limits. In a series of studies involving middle school and high school math classes, students who were forced to struggle on complex problems before receiving help from teachers outperformed students who received immediate assistance. The authors of these studies summarized their findings in a simple yet elegant statement: Skills come from struggle.

Another study, titled "Why Do Only Some Events Cause Learning During Human Tutoring?", found the answer was straightforward: because most tutors swoop in with answers and support far too early. In surveying different university-level physics tutoring systems, the researchers discovered that "regardless of the tutorial explanations employed, when students were not at an impasse, learning was uncommon." The most effective tutoring systems, on the other hand, all shared one thing: They delayed

* Grade level and subject have been changed to protect the identities of these teachers.

Growth comes at the point of resistance. Skills come from struggle.

instruction until students reached the point of failure. Growth comes at the point of resistance. Skills come from struggle.

The same theme holds true in athletics. Whether it's a runner trying to get faster, a basketball player working on a new move, or a big-wave surfer attempting to master a challenging ride, the greatest gains often follow immense struggle and discomfort.

Nic Lamb is one of the best big-wave surfers in the world. He rides waves that are as tall as four-story buildings. Though his performances on the water seem magical, they are grounded in a meticulous approach to training and a bulletproof mindset that he cultivates day in and day out. When Brad interviewed Lamb for *Outside* magazine, he was especially interested to learn how Lamb prepares himself to face the strongest swells. Lamb's secret lies in making himself uncomfortable. "During training, I seek out and try to ride waves that scare me," Lamb said. "It's only when you step outside your comfort zone that you grow. Being uncomfortable is the path to personal development and growth. It is the opposite of complacency."

Lamb embraces the challenge, seeing failure not as a setback but an opportunity to grow. "If I never pushed the envelope, if I never struggled, I would never get better," he said. If anything, the times that Lamb is supremely challenged or comes up short are often the most valuable. They uncover both physical and psychological weak spots and provide insight into areas he can improve. They fully engage both his brain and body in trying to figure out the problem. And they raise the bar of what Lamb considers possible.

What Waitzkin, students who learn successfully, and Lamb practice is something known as "productive failure." There is broad scientific consensus that the most profound learning occurs when we experience this sort of failure. Rather than simply answering a specific question, it is beneficial to be challenged and even to fail. Failure provides an opportunity to analyze a problem from different angles, pushing us to understand its deep underlying structure and to hone the transferrable skill of problem-solving itself. Sure, immediate assistance can be highly satisfying. But when we succumb to the impulse for instant resolution, we miss out on a special kind of deep learning that only a challenge can spawn.

SYSTEM 2 LEARNING

Nobel Prize–winning psychologist Daniel Kahneman, PhD, states that the human mind is divided into two types of thinking: System 1 and System 2. System 1 operates automatically and quickly. It is often driven by instinct and intuition. System 2, on the other hand, is more thoughtful and analytical and addresses effortful mental activities. System 1 is our default mode of thinking, because it requires less energy. When we are on autopilot, System 1 is at work and our current mental model of the world dominates. It's only when we activate System 2, by really working hard and struggling to figure something out, that we have the best chance of examining new information critically and integrating it into our web of knowledge. True learning requires System 2.

To understand why System 2 learning is such a challenge, we need to look deep inside the brain. Our actual web of knowledge consists of brain cells called neurons that are linked by axons, which function like fine electrical wires in the brain. When we learn something new, electrical activity travels between neurons along these axons. At first, the connections are weak (both figuratively and literally) and we struggle with the new skill, whether it's properly using grammar or using our nondominant hand on the basketball court. If we give in, opting not to struggle, System 1 takes over. We default to the already strong connections in our brain and continue using adjectives instead of adverbs or dribbling with our right hand instead of our left. But if we endure the struggle and keep working at the new skill, the connections between neurons strengthen. This occurs partially thanks to a substance called myelin. Myelin is like the brain's version of insulation, wrapping around our axons. As we work more at something, more myelin is generated, and that enables electrical activity to travel more fluidly between neurons. In other words, the connections in our brain

Just like struggling to eke out one last repetition in the weight room is a great method for growing the body, struggling to the point of failure, and only then receiving assistance, is a great recipe for growing the mind.

strengthen. Over time, our former struggles become second nature.

If we stick at learning something for long enough, what was once a formidable System 2 challenge becomes a simple System 1 task. Just ask anyone who learned how to dribble with her nondominant hand. Or, just ask yourself: What does 3 + 2 equal? How about 6 × 4?

Think back. Answering these questions wasn't always so easy.

This is not to say that aimless struggle promotes learning. But it does mean that the best learning occurs when we really have to work for it. Just like struggling to eke out one last repetition in the weight room is a great method for growing the body, struggling to the point of failure and only then receiving assistance is a great recipe for growing the mind. If you want to continuously improve in whatever it is that you do, you've got to view stress as something positive, even desirable. Although too much or never-ending stress can be dangerous, the right amount serves as a powerful stimulus for growth.

PERFORMANCE PRACTICES

- Stress stimulates growth.
- As the chess prodigy turned martial arts champion Josh Waitzkin says, "growth comes at the point of resistance."
- Developing a new capability requires effort: Skills come from struggle.
- When you struggle, System 2 is activated and true development is underway; myelin is accumulating and neural connections are strengthening.
- Fail productively: Only seek out support after you've allowed yourself to struggle.

JUST-MANAGEABLE CHALLENGES

When psychologist Mihaly Csikszentmihalyi, PhD, was studying how the best performers get in the zone and continuously improve, he noticed they all regularly pushed themselves to their limits, and perhaps just a bit beyond. In an attempt to convert the mystical "zone" into something a bit less nebulous, Csikszentmihalyi developed an elegant conceptual tool.

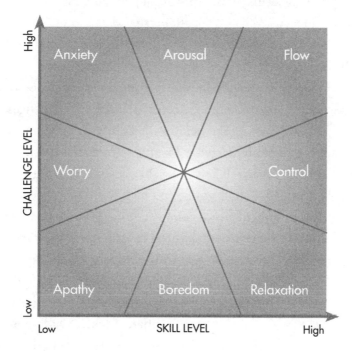

Csikszentmihalyi's tool not only can help you find your way into the zone, but it can also double as a great way to dial in the optimal amount of stress required for growth. The best kind of stress, what we like to call "just-manageable challenges," lies in the upper right corner of the "flow" section.

Just-manageable challenges manifest when you take on something that makes you feel a little out of control but not quite anxious or overly aroused.* When the task at hand is a bit beyond your skills you're in the

---

* Brad first heard the term "just-manageable change" from his undergraduate school professor, Richard Price, PhD, at the University of Michigan.

What you're after is the sweet spot: when the challenge at hand is on the outer edge of, or perhaps just beyond, your current skills.

sweet spot. Any less of a challenge and you'd feel like "I've got this in the bag." It'd be too easy and not stressful enough to serve as a stimulus for growth. Any more of a challenge, however, and the unnerving feeling of your heartbeat pounding in your ears would make it hard to focus. What you're after is the sweet spot: when the challenge at hand is on the outer edge of, or perhaps just beyond, your current skills.

The workouts that Steve designs for his world-class distance runners such as Sara Hall are prime examples of just-manageable challenges. Prior to finishing near the top of the field in the 2016 World Half Marathon Championships, Hall completed a 15-mile tempo run at a staggering 5:30 per mile pace, ever so slightly faster than she ever had before. These workouts are designed to stretch limits, pushing runners beyond their current abilities. As a result, it's not uncommon for Steve's athletes to show up to practice a bit nervous. Some may even question whether they will be able to complete the workout. While armchair sports psychologists might say this kind of doubt and uncertainty is a negative, Steve has a different take. A little doubt and uncertainty is actually a good thing: It signals that a growth opportunity has emerged.

A little doubt and uncertainty is actually a good thing: It signals that a growth opportunity has emerged.

The little voice inside your head saying, "I can't possibly do this," is actually a sign that you're on the right track. It's your mind trying to pull you back to the familiar path that represents your comfort zone. Just-manageable challenges are about venturing off a known path and going down a slightly more demanding one.

This concept applies to just about anything, whether it's a workout, musical performance, or project at the office. That's the beauty of

Csikszentmihalyi's diagram. You can plot any activity on it. When doing so, it is important to account for the many contextual factors that can make an activity more or less challenging at a given point in time.

External factors could include:

- Weather

- Size of the audience (or stakes of the outcome)

- Prize money

- Deadlines

- The people you're assigned to work with (if a group/team project)

Internal factors could include:

- Other stressors in your life at the time

- Your personal interest in and motivation for the activity

- Your physical and mental health

Consider the activities you engage in on an average day. Where do they fall on Csikszentmihalyi's diagram? Are you pursuing growth in a healthy, sustainable way? We aren't suggesting that you spend *all* of your time immersed in just-manageable challenges. Doing so is probably not very practical. Plus, you still need to recover in between bouts of stress for the effort to be beneficial. What we are suggesting, however, is that for the capabilities you wish to grow—whether they be financial modeling, portrait painting, distance running, or anything in between—you should regularly seek out just-manageable challenges: activities that take you out of your comfort zone and force you to push at the point of resistance for growth.

IN THIS CHAPTER, we explored the benefits of stress, examined why skills come from struggle, and learned what types of activities fall into the category of good, growth-promoting stress—what we call just-manageable challenges. Next, we'll explore the mechanics of how you should go about working on them and explain why so much of the conventional wisdom on "productive" work misses the mark.

Performance Practices

- Think of a skill/capability that you want to grow.
- Assess your current ability to perform this skill/capability.
- Actively seek out challenges that just barely exceed your ability.
- If you feel fully in control, make the next challenge a bit harder.
- If you feel anxious or so aroused that you can't focus, dial things down a notch.

3

STRESS YOURSELF

I n the early 1990s, a behavioral scientist named K. Anders Ericsson, PhD, set out to investigate how people become experts. At the time, prevailing wisdom held that experience was the key. That is, the more time someone spent practicing something, the better they would become at doing that task. Eventually, Ericsson reasoned, an accumulation of experience— perhaps with a little help from the right DNA—culminated in expertise. But not long after Ericsson began his project, an entirely different story emerged.

Ericsson discovered obscure research showing that physics professors at the University of California, Berkeley, failed to consistently outperform students on introductory problem sets. Yet some of these professors had been researching and teaching physics for decades. Something didn't add up.

As Ericsson continued digging up little-known studies, he continued to find surprising results. The number of years a psychologist had under his belt, for example, had no correlation to how successful he was at treating patients. Other research showed that many physicians actually got *worse* at making diagnoses from radiographic scans as they *gained* more experience. The more time that passed since their formal training, the more errors they made. In every field that's been studied (from wine tasting to financial investing), when it came to differentiating top performers, experience was not the critical variable. In some cases, it was nearly impossible for Ericsson to distinguish between the performances of novices and long-time veterans. Regardless of what angle he examined it from, Ericsson found experience and expertise did not necessarily go hand in hand.

So, Ericsson wondered, if not experience, then what is it that makes someone an expert? To find out, he and a team of researchers traveled to Berlin, Germany, and embedded themselves among violinists at the illustrious Global Music Academy. The academy had an international reputation for training violinists; many of the world's best passed through the Global Music Academy's hallowed doors. When Ericsson and his team arrived, they asked the violinists to continue doing exactly what they had been doing, with only one small exception: write it all down. At the end of each day, the violinists recorded how they spent each and every one of their waking minutes. After a 7-day period, Ericsson compared the diaries of the top performers—those whom professors at the academy said were good enough to have careers as international soloists—to everyone else. Nearly everyone practiced the same amount of time each week: roughly 50 hours. This didn't surprise Ericsson in the slightest. Simply being invited to the Global Music Academy required immense dedication and hard work. Plus, that all the violinists practiced the same amount of time only confirmed what Ericsson already knew—experience alone doesn't make an expert.

Next, the researchers examined what was happening in those 50 hours. How was everyone practicing? The answer was: quite differently. The best violinists spent significantly more time intensely focused on mastering a specific goal, and remained totally present when doing so. They eliminated all distractions. They rarely, if ever, merely went through the motions. The best violinists were practicing, as Ericsson and his team coined it, far more "deliberately" than everyone else.

Ericsson and his research team went on to conduct additional studies on athletes, artists, and intellectuals. They found the same thing every time: It isn't experience that sets top performers apart but the amount of deliberate prac-

> *It isn't experience that sets top performers apart but the amount of deliberate practice they put in. Practice doesn't make perfect. Perfect practice makes perfect.*

tice they put in. Although Ericsson would become associated with the Malcolm Gladwell–popularized 10,000-hour rule—the notion that anyone can become an expert at anything by practicing for 10,000 hours—his *actual* findings represent something quite different. Expertise is not about a certain number of hours practiced. Rather, it's about the type of work that fills those hours. Practice doesn't make perfect. Perfect practice makes perfect.

PERFECT PRACTICE

So what exactly makes perfect practice? Ericsson found that top performers actively seek out just-manageable challenges, setting goals for practice sessions that just barely exceed their current capabilities. But that is only half the story. What really differentiates deliberate practice is deep concentration.

To test this, researchers took a group of professional and amateur singers and hooked them up to devices that measure physiological indicators of focus. Once the sensors were in place, the singers went through their usual practice routines. At the end, each singer was asked a handful of questions to assess his level of comfort and focus. A clear pattern emerged. Both the hard physiological data and the soft self-reported data showed that, for the amateur singers, the practice session released tension and was generally enjoyable. The professional singers, on the other hand, demonstrated large increases in concentration throughout the practice session. They focused carefully on improving specific parts of their performance—even if that made the session less enjoyable. The best singers were stretching a bit

Across the board, when great performers are doing serious work their bodies and minds are 100 percent there. They are fully engaged in the moment.

beyond their comfort zones and doing so with keen awareness. Though the amateurs and the professionals practiced for the same amount of time, the way in which they used that time was quite different.

Across the board, when great performers are doing serious work their bodies and minds are 100 percent there. They are fully engaged in the moment.

FULLY PRESENT

One of our mentors is a man named Bob Kocher, MD. He is the definition of a Renaissance man. His formal training is in medicine. He went to undergraduate school at the University of Washington and medical school at George Washington University. Although he didn't go to a top Ivy like Harvard or Yale, he was awarded the extremely elite Howard Hughes Medical Institute Fellowship, the equivalent to a Rhodes Scholarship in medicine. He practiced as a physician at the Harvard-affiliated Beth Israel Deaconess Medical Center, but after a few years Dr. Bob (as pretty much everyone calls him) realized he could not fully help ailing patients because he was operating in an ailing system. It was a tough and scary decision, but he made the difficult choice to transition out of clinical practice in search of opportunities to make health care better on a systematic level. He found plenty.

Since hanging up his white coat, Dr. Bob has worn many hats: partner at a major consulting firm; health care economist reporting directly to the president of the United States; scholar at the Brookings Institution; and professor at Stanford University, to name just a few. Currently, he is a partner at one of Silicon Valley's largest venture capital firms, where he invests millions of dollars in start-up companies with products and services that are potential game-changers in health care. His opinions on innovation and health care are published in the *New York Times* and prestigious academic journals. Dr. Bob has been interviewed as an expert for countless bestselling books. When national, and even international, leaders are forced to make decisions about health care, they often wait until they've spoken with him. Long story short: Dr. Bob is a top performer if there ever was one.

Of course we admire Dr. Bob for all of these achievements and the hard work that they rest upon. But we also look up to him because he wears a $40 digital watch; that is to say, he doesn't do any of this for the money, nor is he driven by material glitz. He prioritizes his physical health, exercising for at least an hour nearly every day. Most important, he is a wonderful husband and father of two young girls, almost always home in time for dinner, and present at extracurricular activities. So when we met with Dr. Bob at his Palo Alto office, what we wanted to learn most is how— how does he accomplish so much while seemingly maintaining balance in his life? He answered our question without needing to say a word.

From the minute we walked into the room with Dr. Bob, we were in the room with Dr. Bob. We were not in the room with Dr. Bob's email, phone, or any interrupting colleagues. Prior to our time together he was crafting an article for a high-profile medical journal and making decisions about the future of a company. But he didn't bring those issues into the room with us either. It was just the three of us discussing this book. The energy was palpable. He gave us the same attention he gives to the president of the United States. Dr. Bob was fully present. We were witnessing in real time his secret to success.

By doing one thing at a time and devoting his full concentration to that one thing, Dr. Bob is able to do many things well—from writing and influencing health care policy, to investing in companies, to being a good husband and father. His insistence on single-tasking ensures that he learns and grows from every document he drafts

> *By doing one thing at a time and devoting his full concentration to that one thing, Dr. Bob is able to do many things well.*

and every interaction he's involved in. "It's not that I can't multitask," he says. "But when I do multitask everything suffers. So I just don't multitask. Ever."

He compartmentalizes his day down to the hour. Each compartment has a concrete objective. These objectives range from, for example: write 500 words for a paper; learn enough about a company to make an investment decision; have a free-flowing conversation with an interesting person; keep his heart rate at 80 percent of its maximum in a fitness class; influence a decision maker in a highly political meeting; enjoy dinner with his wife and kids. This type of compartmentalization ensures he follows his governing rule: "Do only one thing at a time." Dr. Bob's secret to doing so much is doing so little. He is the ultimate single-tasker.

SINGLE-TASKING

Dr. Bob's story is insightful, but does his strategy hold true for everyone? And if it does, then why do so many people insist on multitasking?

We love multitasking because when we do multiple things at once, we feel more productive and experience greater emotional satisfaction. An internal voice in our subconscious mind says, "Look at everything I am accomplishing. Look at all of the boxes I am checking off my list." In a society that encourages and rewards "optimization" and "multiple processes," we can't help but want to "optimize" ourselves.

> *For 99 percent of us, effective multitasking is nothing more than effective delusional thinking.*

Unfortunately, our brains don't work like computers. For 99 percent of us,* effective multitasking is nothing more than effective delusional thinking.

Even in individuals who claim to be great multitaskers, fMRI scans of the brain reveal it is impossible to do two things at once with a high level of quality. When we multitask, our brains either constantly switch

---

* Studies show that a little over 1 percent of the population can effectively multitask. Odds are you aren't in that 1 percent. That's just how odds work.

between tasks or they divide and conquer, allotting only a portion of our cognitive capacity to a specific task. As a result, as countless studies show, the quality and, ironically, even the quantity of our work suffers when we are multitasking.

Although the switching costs may seem trivial—sometimes just a few tenths of a second per switch—they add up over time as we switch back-and-forth between tasks. Researchers at the University of Michigan found that seemingly innocuous multitasking can cannibalize as much as 40 percent of someone's productive time. Although it may feel like we are getting twice as much done when multitasking, we're *actually* getting close to half as much done.

It's not just our short-term performance that suffers at the hands of multitasking. Additional research shows that people who are "chronic" multitaskers are worse at filtering out irrelevant information, slower at identifying patterns, and have worse long-term memories. In other words, multitasking not only makes the work we do today suffer, but it also makes the work we'll do tomorrow suffer. As Ericsson's expert violinists and the Renaissance man Dr. Bob all demonstrate, engaging in a task with singular focus is how we grow from stress.

PERFORMANCE PRACTICES

Apply the components of perfect practice each time you set out to do meaningful work:

- Define a purpose and concrete objectives for each working session.
- Ask yourself: What do I want to learn or get done?
- Focus and concentrate deeply, even if doing so isn't always enjoyable.
- Single-task: The next time you feel like multitasking, remind yourself that research shows it's not effective. Keep in mind Dr. Bob's secret: "Do only one thing at a time."
- Remember that quality trumps quantity.

Unfortunately, simply knowing the perils of multitasking doesn't mean we'll stop doing it. The technologies that enable and facilitate multitasking can be addicting. They take us out of full engagement, decreasing the potential growth stimulus of whatever it is we are doing. (Just imagine if a runner doing intervals on the track came to a complete stop to check her phone after each and every notification. The constant start-and-stop would certainly impair her performance.) But before we can figure out effective ways to escape the pull of these technologies, we must first understand why we have become so addicted to them in the first place.

ADDICTED TO OUR SMARTPHONES

If we had to bet on it (more on that in a minute), we'd wager that you love your phone. There's nothing wrong with that. We love our phones, too. They are incredible gadgets that enable a level of connectivity no one could have dreamed of even 15 years ago. As a matter of fact, if we didn't love our phones, you probably wouldn't be reading this book right now. In early 2014, Brad scrolled down on his Twitter feed from a sidewalk in downtown San Francisco and saw an intriguing tweet from a guy named Steve Magness who, at the time, was at a coffee shop in Houston. Brad clicked the link in Steve's tweet and became excited about what he was reading. As he read, Brad was floored, thinking: "Wow, seems like this guy and I are on the same wavelength about a lot of stuff." Brad read a few more of Steve's blog posts and decided he had to shoot Steve a quick email. A few minutes and a few scroll-downs later, Steve, from his phone, two time zones away, hit "reply." And just like that, a fruitful connection was formed.

Needless to say, we are not here to demonize technology. But because of stories like ours, and some clever, if not manipulative, design on the part of digital app makers, many of us love our smartphones so much that we simply can't resist them. They are so addictive that each and every day hundreds of people risk and lose their lives because of them. According to the Centers for Disease Control and Prevention (CDC), more than nine people are killed and more than 1,150 people are injured *daily* in automobile crashes that involve a distracted driver. In a recent survey, 31 percent of US drivers ages 18 to 64 said that at least once in the past 30 days they had engaged in the most dangerous type of distracted driving there is: texting (or tweeting, emailing, Facebooking, etc.). Unfortunately, many believe this number is significantly under-reported. Have an honest moment with yourself. In the past 30 days, have you checked your phone and/or texted from it while driving? If you haven't, have you been a passenger in the car of a driver who has? If you answered no to both questions, that's great. But we're afraid you are in the minority. Although the dangers are well known, most of us simply can't fight the urge to check our phones.

To unravel why this is the case, let's turn to another addiction that ruins many lives: gambling. When a gambler awaits their next card at the blackjack table or pulls down the lever on a slot machine, they get a hit of the powerful neurochemical dopamine. Dopamine excites and arouses us. Under the influence of dopamine, we feel revved up and alive. Unlike other neurochemicals that are released when we've achieved something, the far more potent dopamine is released prior to the payoff of an event, when we are longing for or desiring something deeply. In other words, we don't become addicted to winning; we become addicted to the chase.

The unpredictability of gambling—the feeling we get while we wait for the dealer to turn over his card or for the slots to cease spinning—triggers a super-sized dopamine rush. That's because uncertain situations, when there is a mere *chance* of winning, are far more irresistible than situations in which we know we'll win every time. If this weren't the case, then people would get all jazzed up about putting their money into municipal bonds with guaranteed 4 percent returns instead of into slot machines. But alas, the brain rewards us with more dopamine for the act of seeking a reward than for the act of receiving one.

While being biochemically drawn to the chase is not a survival advantage in modern-day casinos, long ago it was a necessity. If it wasn't for our attraction to unpredictable rewards, we wouldn't be here today. Our earliest ancestors needed a compelling reason to endure days-long hunts for food with no guarantee of success. So we evolved to crave the chase.

This same tendency explains why, thousands of years later, we can't put down our phones. Our phones and the apps on them, designed by highly sophisticated PhDs to lure us in, operate like slot machines. When we swipe down and wait for our email and instant messenger and Twitter and Facebook and Instagram and on and on to refresh, dopamine floods our system. Instead of a row of cherries or 7s, the potential rewards we are chasing are new likes, comments, or messages. Although most of us aren't rewarded every time we check our phone, we are rewarded often enough to keep us checking. And since there is always a chance that someone somewhere is pinging us, we can't stop using our social slot machines. Even when we're on the highway. This isn't only a problem when it comes to safe driving. It's also a problem when it comes to performance. Because, as we discussed earlier, the most effective work—the kind that yields greatness and growth—demands our entire focus. When we met with Dr. Bob, he didn't check his phone once. He didn't even think about it. It wasn't even in the room.

OUT OF SIGHT, OUT OF MIND

The most common defense against smartphone distraction is straightforward: turn your phone to silent mode and then place it face down on the table, or perhaps even put it in your pocket. Unfortunately, this alone won't enable you to engage in the deep focus necessary for peak performance. Telling someone they can keep their cell phone within arm's reach but cannot check it is not much different than telling a drug addict he can keep a loaded syringe in plain sight but may not use it. In both cases, the craving for reward, and the emotional and chemical addiction to it, is overpowering.

Resisting the temptation to check our phones is only made harder by the tricks our minds play on us. Have you ever had your phone turned off in your pocket, only to feel it vibrate nevertheless? If so, you're not alone. A recent study from Indiana University–Purdue University Fort Wayne found that 89 percent of college students suffer from "phantom vibration syndrome." About once every 2 weeks, college students reported they felt their phone vibrating when it wasn't. Although they knew their phones were off, their subconscious longing for a notification manifested in a physical sensation. They stopped whatever they were doing to check their buzzing phones that weren't really buzzing.

Let's say that you could somehow resist the temptation to check your phone when it is near you. This in and of itself would take a lot of effort. Rather than devoting all your cognitive energy to what you are truly trying to accomplish, a good portion of it instead goes toward thinking about checking your phone, imagining what might be awaiting you on it, and restraining yourself from actually checking. For a study published in *The Journal of Social Psychology*, researchers asked a group of college students to complete a series of difficult motor tasks when their cell phones were visible. Sure enough, their performance was significantly worse than a control group where participants' cell phones were not visible. Things got even more interesting when all the participants' cell phones were removed but the study leader's cell phone remained present. Incredibly, even when the phone visible wasn't their own, study participants' performance suffered.

Smartphones distract us whether they are on, off, in our pockets, or on a table, and they command our attention even when they are not our own. Though it pains us (i.e., Brad and Steve) to say, odds are that just reading about smartphones for the past few minutes may have distracted you from this text. Perhaps this discussion even prompted you to feel for your phone or, worse, check it. It follows that the best solution for preventing smartphone distraction is to remove it from the picture altogether. It turns out there is a lot of truth in the expression "out of sight, out of mind."

Walter Mischel, PhD, is a world-renowned expert on willpower at

> *Smartphones distract us whether they are on, off, in our pockets, or on a tables and they command our attention even when they are not our own. The best solution for preventing smartphone distraction is to remove it from the picture altogether.*

Columbia University. He's devoted over 30 years to exploring how and why some people are able to resist temptation and others are not. In his years of research, across numerous studies involving children and adults, Mischel has found that one of the best methods for self-control is to move the object of desire out of view. (Or in the case of vibrating phones, perhaps "out of feel.") Mischel's findings explain why recovering gamblers are prohibited from being near casinos and why dieters have long been told to keep unhealthy foods hidden in hard-to-access places or outside the house altogether. The mere sight of a desirable object triggers dopamine, which is like the devil on our shoulder that says, "Are you sure you don't want to have just one?"

While writing this chapter, Brad began testing "out of sight, out of mind" in a number of situations in his own life. Whether he was doing hard intervals on the elliptical trainer, lifting weights, or writing this book, his performance improved when his smartphone was completely removed from the picture. Real and objective performance measures for each activity—such as watts generated, pounds lifted, and words written—all increased. This objective data supported what he subjectively experienced. Without his smartphone visible, Brad quickly forgot about its existence. He felt as if he had another 10 to 15 percent of effort to give to the task at hand. Not having the option of turning on his phone and looking at it did far more than lift a small weight out of his pocket. It felt like a huge weight had been lifted off his shoulders.

PERFORMANCE PRACTICES

- Identify what interrupts your deep focus. Common intruders, many of which are enabled by smartphones, include:

  - ✓ Text messages
  - ✓ Social media
  - ✓ The internet
  - ✓ Television

- Remove distractors: Remember that only out of sight truly leads to out of mind.

BLOCKS OF STRESS

Stressing yourself is tiring. Great performers understand and respect that there is a limit to how much stress they can tolerate. They are aware that if they exceed this limit, then good, productive stress can become harmful and toxic.

In his years of studying experts, Ericsson found that top performers across all fields are unable to sustain intense work and deep concentration for more than 2 hours. Outside of rare, short-term situations, once this threshold is passed, neither the body nor the mind can sustain the workload. Great performers, Ericsson found, generally work in chunks of 60 to 90 minutes separated by short breaks.

While Ericsson's work focused predominantly on creatives (e.g., artists) and competitors (e.g., chess players and athletes), new research shows his conclusions also hold true in the workplace. Recently, an international social networking company called the Draugiem Group wanted to uncover what habits set apart their most successful workers. To do so, they partnered with the makers of DeskTime, a time-tracking app sophisticated enough to distinguish between when employees are working and when they are not. The Draugiem Group found that their all-star workers adhered to a particular routine: They spent 52 minutes engrossed in their work before taking a 17-minute break.

Similar to the Draugiem Group, other companies have manipulated and analyzed their employees' work. Without fail, regardless of industry or job description, chunks of hard work followed by short breaks yielded the best performance. The most productive workers in a meat processing plant worked in hourly cycles of 51 minutes on and 9 minutes off. Agricultural workers performed best when they worked in 90-minute cycles of 75 minutes on and 15 minutes off. Other studies examining the habits of workers performing highly demanding cognitive work found cycling between 50 minutes of work and 7 minutes of recovery generated the best output.

While the exact work-to-rest ratio depends on the demands of the job and individual preferences, the overall theme is clear: alternating between blocks of 50 to 90 minutes of intense work and recovery breaks of 7 to

Alternating between blocks of 50 to 90 minutes of intense work and recovery breaks of 7 to 20 minutes enables people to sustain the physical, cognitive, and emotional energy required for peak performance.

20 minutes enables people to sustain the physical, cognitive, and emotional energy required for peak performance. This ebb and flow runs counter to the all-too-common constant grind of either perpetually working in an "in-between zone" of moderately hard work or working at the utmost intensity nonstop. Neither of these more traditional approaches is ideal. The former leads to under-performance. The latter leads to physical, cognitive, and emotional fatigue and, eventually, burnout.

One data entry company that was experiencing employee burnout inserted into every hour mandatory breaks of at least 5 minutes, plus two additional longer breaks throughout the day. Even though they "gave away" about an hour of paid work, total output per employee remained unchanged. More important, employee discomfort and eye strain were significantly reduced. By working smart—that is to say, alternating between blocks of hard work followed by short breaks—we get the most out of ourselves and avoid crippling fatigue and burnout.

It is interesting to note that in the world of elite running, this is old news. In the 1930s, when German running coach Woldemar Gerschler first developed interval training, or intense repetitions of running with short breaks in between, the objective was simple: enable a runner to accomplish the greatest possible amount of high-quality work before fatigue caused performance to suffer. Nearly a century later, Steve and just about every other top running coach still rely upon intervals to increase the amount of quality work their athletes can execute. And, although it's taken nearly 100 years, it's nice to see that progressive employers are finally beginning to realize the value of intervals off the track.

Much like it takes time for a runner to build the fitness necessary to execute high-intensity intervals, it may take time to build yourself up to blocks of undistracted work. This is especially true for people who are

---

PERFORMANCE PRACTICES

- Divide your work into chunks of 50 to 90 minutes (this may vary by task). Start even smaller if you find yourself struggling to maintain attention.

- As you develop "fitness" in whatever it is you are doing, you'll likely find that you can work longer and harder.

- For most activities and most situations, 2 hours should be the uppermost limit for a working block.

---

accustomed to multitasking or working amid digital-device distraction. If you find yourself struggling to maintain full attention (e.g., checking your smartphone for notifications, pulling up your email browser, mind-wandering), start with small chunks of 10 to 15 minutes and gradually increase the duration every week. No different from any other skill, deep work is a practice that must be cultivated over time.

MINDSET MATTERS

Imagine you just finished a hard, physical outdoor workout on a scorching summer day. Someone presents you with an ice-cold milkshake. Hot and hungry as you might be, before indulging, you might ask: What's in the shake? Is it a healthy, low-calorie blend of organic fruits and vegetables with almond milk and whey protein? Or is it the nutritional opposite: a calorie bomb of full-fat chocolate ice cream, whole milk, and sugary syrup?

Science (and common sense) tells us that our bodies would react differently to each of these drinks. The calorie bomb would, at first, make us feel more satiated. A few hours later, however, thanks to all the sugar, we'd crave more sweets. The healthy version, on the other hand, would refresh and energize us, leaving us feeling lighter on our feet. But it may also leave us a bit less satisfied than if we'd gone for the other option. Perhaps we'd find ourselves snacking sooner.

When researchers from Yale compared how people responded to the two shakes just described, they confirmed all of these assumptions. Study participants who received the unhealthy shake reported feeling greater immediate satisfaction but craved more sweets later. They also experienced a steeper decline in ghrelin. Ghrelin is the hormone associated with hunger, and its decline told their brains that "I'm full." None of this should sound surprising, because it's not—it's precisely what you'd expect to happen. With one small exception: The contents of the milkshakes given to each group were exactly the same. The only thing that differed was the description. It was the participants' minds—not the sugar, fat, fruits, vegetables, or protein—that controlled not only how they subjectively felt after drinking the shakes, but also their deep hormonal response.

It's easy to dismiss the impact of "mindsets" as a pop-psychology concept aimed at making us feel better about ourselves, but the hard science tells a different story. The lens through which we view the world affects everything from learning to health to longevity to our hormonal response to "different" milkshakes.

GET YOUR MIND RIGHT

In the late 1960s at Yale University, a young PhD candidate named Carol Dweck was studying helplessness in children. In particular, she wanted to answer the question: Why do some children give up when faced with failure, while others are motivated by it? The answer, she found, was all in their heads.

The children who gave up easily also avoided challenges and felt threatened by others who were different from themselves. They often perceived learning and growth as outside of their control. In their minds, the qualities that determined whether they would succeed or fail were fixed. In adult-speak, these children believed it was their innate ability and talent— their genetic code—that governed the outcome of nearly all situations in life. To them, they either "had it" or they didn't. They were either smart or stupid. The children who were motivated by and more apt to confront challenges, on the other hand, had a completely different mindset. They felt that with hard work they could do anything. They didn't see ability as something that was fixed, but rather as something that could be improved with practice over time. These children had what Dweck called a "growth mindset."

When Dweck and her colleagues tracked the performance of a group of seventh-grade students for 2 years, they found that although all the students started from the same measurable baseline, those with growth mindsets progressed significantly faster than their fixed-mindset peers. The growth-mindset students were willing to push themselves harder, sought out just-manageable challenges, and viewed productive failure as a positive. In contrast, the fixed-mindset students avoided challenges and quit when the going got tough.

It may seem that the mindset we develop is largely out of our control, resulting from the values instilled by our parents, caregivers, and perhaps very first teachers we encountered at a young age. Were we rewarded for hard work and effort (growth-mindset promoting)? Or were we rewarded only for outcomes (fixed-mindset promoting)? Furthermore, by the very nature of a fixed mindset, are those who have fixed mindsets inherently stuck with them? Or is there a way to change people's minds?

To find out, Dweck put seventh-grade students with fixed mindsets through an 8-week course that focused on neuroplasticity, or the science of how the brain can grow. The curriculum included convincing studies and captivating stories that worked together to show students how flexible their minds really are. It worked. At the end of the course, the vast majority of students who had previously felt that their abilities were fixed shifted their outlooks. More important, their rate of progression in school increased. Remarkably, as they shifted their mindset they also shifted their academic trajectory, going from near-failure to academic success.

Dweck's work proved that the way we think about the world has a profound effect on what we do in it. If we cultivate a growth mindset

The way we think about the world has a profound effect on what we do in it.

and believe that skills come from struggle, then we are more likely to expose ourselves to the good kind of growth-promoting stress. But the power of mindsets doesn't stop there. It turns out that our mindset toward stress not only determines if we'll expose ourselves to it, but also how we'll respond.

CHALLENGE RESPONSE

When you hear the word "stress," what comes to mind? Maybe you thought about growth. If you didn't, don't feel bad. Even though the first section of this book has highlighted the positive attributes of stress, it still might be hard for you to overcome years of being told that stress is toxic. Culture has conditioned us to minimize stress and avoid it at all costs. For the unfortunate times when we can't avoid stress, we are given "coping" techniques or strategies to "get through it" so that we can "minimize the damage." Even we, Brad and Steve, in the middle of writing a chapter extolling the virtues of stress, experienced a negative kneejerk reaction to the word. This is an unfortunate and costly bias that is difficult to overcome.

Kelly McGonigal, PhD, is a health psychologist at Stanford University. For many years, like every other health psychologist, she worked tirelessly to help people avoid stress. Her outlook was this: Stress is bad and her job was to figure out how people could minimize its negative impact. But then she came across research that blew her mind.

A 2010 study found that the small portion of Americans who view stress as facilitative have a 43 percent lower chance of premature death than those who view stress as destructive. The obvious explanation, or course, is that the people with a positive outlook toward stress developed that mindset because they didn't experience stress very often. That is, if you're never feeling stressed, then of course you would think that stress isn't so bad. But when the researchers compared the total number of stressful events that each group experienced, they were shocked to discover that the number was virtually the same. Researchers controlled for just about every variable besides mindset and still saw significant mortality differences. Could something as simple as one's attitude about stress truly contribute to extending life?

This question captivated McGonigal. Might she possibly have had it wrong for all these years? Her quest to find the

How we view stress weighs heavily on how stress influences us.

answer turned into *The Upside of Stress*, a book that challenged the prevailing wisdom on stress. She discovered a large body of evidence showing that how we view stress weighs heavily on how stress influences us.

Some individuals learn to assess stressors as challenges rather than threats. This outlook, which researchers call a "challenge response," is characterized by viewing stress as something productive, and, much like we've written, as a stimulus for growth. In the midst of stress, those who demonstrate a challenge response proactively focus on what they can control. With this outlook, negative emotions like fear and anxiety decrease. This response better enables these individuals to manage and even thrive under stress. But that's not all. Just like our mindset about milkshakes changes our deep biological profile, so, too, does our mindset about stress.

Of the many hormones at play when we are stressed, two are particularly important: cortisol and dehydroepiandrosterone (DHEA). While neither is categorically "good" or "bad" and both are necessary, chronically elevated cortisol levels are associated with lingering inflammation, impaired immune function, and depression. By contrast, DHEA has been linked to a reduced risk of anxiety, depression, heart disease, neurodegeneration, and a range of other diseases and conditions. DHEA is also a neurosteroid, which helps the brain grow. When under stress, you want to release more DHEA than cortisol. This ratio is aptly named the "growth index of stress." Sure enough, studies show that people who react to stress with a challenge response have a higher growth index of stress versus those who perceive stress as a threat. In other words, if you frame stressors as challenges, you'll release more DHEA than cortisol. As a result your growth index of stress will be higher, and you'll actually experience health *benefits* instead of health detriments. And, according to the 2010 study on stress and mortality that we mentioned earlier, you might just live longer, too.

It's becoming clear that cultivating a growth mindset and a challenge response to stress is highly beneficial. These mindsets increase our health and longevity. And, as we're about to learn, they also enhance our performance.

HOW THE BEST VIEW STRESS

At the start of an Olympic event, most of the athletes share a look of stoic, steely-eyed determination. Few, if any, Olympians appear to be anxious. Contrast this with your local 5-K race, where weekend warriors trying to run at an 8-minute-per-mile pace are nervous and stressed out . . . all while racing for a finisher's medal they'll be given regardless of their performance. What's going on here? Are the elites simply immune to stress? Of course not. They just know how to channel it effectively.

In a study including more than 200 elite and nonelite swimmers, researchers used a psychological survey (the Competitive State Anxiety Inventory) to measure stress before a major race, and then asked each athlete if they viewed stress as beneficial or harmful. They found that prior to the race, both the elite and nonelite swimmers experienced the same intensity of cognitive and physical stress. They all felt the nerves, anxiousness, and perhaps even a bit of fear that accompanies standing at the edge of a pool awaiting the starter's gun and the impending world of hurt that follows it. The difference was that the nonelites viewed stress as something to avoid, ignore, and try to quiet. They felt stress would hurt their performance. The elites, on the other hand, interpreted the stress and the sensations that came with it as an aid to their performance; it prepared them to get the most out of their bodies. In other words, the elites exhibited a challenge response to stress, and, as a result, it didn't bother them nearly as much. If anything, it helped them channel their heightened physiological arousal into explosiveness in the pool.

Additional research, published in the *Journal of Experimental Psychology*, shows that instead of trying to calm yourself down, "reappraising pre-performance anxiety as excitement" is often advantageous. When you try to suppress pre-event nerves, you are inherently telling yourself that something is wrong. Not only does this make the situation worse, but it also takes emotional and physical energy to fight off the feeling of anxiety—energy that could be better spent on the task at hand. Fortunately, according to the authors of this paper, simply telling yourself "I am excited" shifts your demeanor from what they call a threat mindset (stressed out and apprehensive) to an opportunity mindset (revved up and ready to go). "Compared to those who attempt to calm down," the authors conclude, "individuals who reappraise their anxious arousal as excitement perform better." Put differently: The sensations you feel prior to a big event are neutral—if you view them in a positive light, they are more likely to have a positive impact on your performance.

These studies confirm what every great performer we interviewed for this book told us. They all admitted to feeling stress, especially prior to big performances. But they also all said that rather than try to push the stress away, they welcome and channel it toward the task at hand. In the words of world champion whitewater kayaker Dane Jackson, "Fear [perhaps the most potent form of stress] is there for me in every aspect of kayaking, whether I'm preparing for a run on the biggest waterfall or before my final ride at the world championships. I don't hide from it or try to ignore it. I feel the sensation and channel it to help me focus, to nail the line or to put up the biggest ride I can."

> *By pushing us toward just-manageable challenges and enhancing how we'll respond to them, the right mindset opens up the possibility for growth to occur.*

Mindset research doesn't suggest that innate ability doesn't matter, but it does suggest that how we nurture our nature matters, too. By pushing us toward just-manageable challenges and enhancing how we'll respond to them, the right mindset opens up the possibility for growth to occur.

IN THE LAST TWO CHAPTERS, we focused on the first half of the growth equation: stress. We explored how stress, when it is at the right dose, serves as a powerful stimulus for growth; how skills come from struggle and productive failure; and the value of actively seeking out just-manageable challenges. We also learned how to stress ourselves: in blocks that last under 2 hours, with deep focus, deliberate practice, and with our digital devices out of the picture. Finally, we saw how our mindset affects not only how we perceive stress, but also how we respond to it.

Although allowing ourselves to be stressed and doing so with a growth mindset can feel hard, it turns out that might actually be the easy part. In a paradoxical twist, the second half of the growth equation, rest, can be even harder. Ernest Hemingway said that as difficult as his blocks of writing were, it was "the wait until the next day," when he forced himself to rest, that was hardest to get through. Or, in the words of another great author, Stephen King, "For me, not working is the real work."

Next, we'll turn to the second half of the growth equation. The work of not working. Rest.

PERFORMANCE PRACTICES

- Remember the power of mindset: How you view something fundamentally changes how your body responds to it.

- In situations when you feel the sensation of stress, remind yourself this is your body's natural way of preparing for a challenge; take a deep breath and channel the heightened arousal and sharper perception toward the task at hand.

- Challenge yourself to view stress productively, and even to welcome it. You'll not only perform better, you'll also improve your health.

4

THE PARADOX
OF REST

ne of our friends, Adam*, is an engineer on Google's self-driving car project (now its own division, called Waymo). He says the daily pace of work borders on fanatical. When he's in the lab, the outside world disappears—we know this because he tells us so, and also because our text messages and emails to him almost always go unanswered. Adam works full tilt, wholly immersing himself in the brains and guts of a car that, if Google gets it right, will be a total game-changer. Adam, however, would never say that. He knows that he and his team must first figure out, among many other things, how to teach an inanimate object moving at 70 miles per hour to differentiate between a stray plastic bag and a stray deer. Talk about a just-manageable challenge . . .

Google is built upon projects like the self-driving car: endeavors that push at the point of resistance for growth, where struggle and productive

---

* Name has been changed to protect our friend's identity.

failure aren't consequences *of* the work, but rather the driving forces *behind* it. The company attracts the cream of the crop, top-notch creative thinkers who are passionate about what they do. Add to the mix the tight deadlines and the colleagues who aren't scared to push the envelope, and it's easy to see why employees like Adam become so absorbed in their work. Google has nailed the recipe for stress. But the company understands that's only half the battle. Without rest, Google wouldn't end up with innovation. Instead, it'd end up with a workforce that is broken down and burnt out.

Burnout is undoubtedly one of Google's gravest threats, and holding back passionate employees is often a far more formidable challenge than pushing them ahead. Fortunately, Google has brought the same innovative mindset to this dilemma as the company has to all its other projects. But unlike just about everything else that Google does, the company isn't helping its employees rest by looking ahead to cutting-edge technologies. Rather, Google nails rest by looking back to an ancient Eastern practice.

SEARCH INSIDE YOURSELF

In the early days of Google, employee #107, Chade-Meng Tan, observed that while he and his colleagues had no problem "turning it on," they struggled mightily to "turn it off." Taking short breaks, let alone disconnecting from work in the evenings and on weekends, was impossible. Even if early Googlers wanted to rest, the pace and thrill of their work made it hard to do. Google was growing fast, but Tan had the wisdom to realize that this style of work—stress without rest—was unsustainable.

At Google, Tan was a software engineer. Outside of work, he was an avid practitioner of mindfulness meditation, a Buddhist style of sitting meditation in which the practitioner focuses solely on the breath. Tan's mindfulness practice helped him to transition from the stress of intense work to a more restful state. He also found that it opened his mind to otherwise hidden insights. Mindfulness, Tan decided, was exactly what Google needed.

So, in 2007, Tan launched Search Inside Yourself, a 7-week mindfulness meditation course for Google employees. At first, his colleagues were reluctant. They questioned what, if anything, a mystical, new-age, candle-lit, deep-chanting practice could do for them. But it wasn't long before Tan's colleagues learned that mindfulness—which of course is none of the things we just mentioned—had the power to change the way they worked and lived. Soon, Googlers who went through Tan's class were raving about its benefits. They felt calmer, clear-headed, and more focused. They were able to unplug at the end of the day and even detach enough so that weekends and vacations became truly rejuvenating.

Word spread quickly through the halls of Google about Search Inside Yourself, and it wasn't long before demand for the course surpassed Tan's ability to teach it, something he was doing in addition to his engineering job. Google's leadership team couldn't help but notice the benefits of Search Inside Yourself, either. Their employees were healthier, happier, and more productive. They approached Tan and asked him if he'd be interested in teaching mindfulness meditation full-time and leading a new department, called Personal Growth. Tan was floored by the offer and took it, with only one condition: his job title would no longer be software engineer. He'd now be called "Jolly Good Fellow."

Search Inside Yourself continued to grow, eventually beyond the walls of Google. Today, the independent Search Inside Yourself Leadership Institute (SIYLI) operates with an expanded mission and teaches mindfulness to individuals in a variety of organizations. Tan remains intimately involved as chairman of the board (though he still prefers his colleagues refer to him as a jolly good fellow), where he leads a staff of 14 full-time employees who are dedicated to spreading the power of mindfulness.

To learn more about mindfulness meditation, we visited SIYLI in San Francisco's Presidio district. There, we met with Brandon Rennels, a mindfulness teacher. Rennels is about 30 years old, but his hair is graying as if to say "the wisdom of mindfulness fills this head." And from what we could gather, it does.

Upon first meeting Rennels, we couldn't help but notice that he is fully present. None of his movements are without intention. He focuses with a deep gaze that soaks up every detail of his surroundings. When we walked into a conference room, presumably one Rennels has been in hundreds of times, he observed the room as if he was walking out onto a ledge to observe the Grand Canyon. The same thing happened when he opened his laptop: He looked like a 4-year-old discovering a MacBook for the first time. Rennels was taking it all in, seemingly awestruck by things we considered ordinary.

Rennels told us that he wasn't always like this. Prior to SIYLI, he worked for a large management consulting firm. Though he was good for the job, an opinion confirmed by promotions and strong performance reviews, the job wasn't good for him. Rennels noticed himself chasing external rewards and craving status. He found it hard to focus—something almost impossible to believe given what we witnessed at SIYLI—and he could never calm his racing mind. He told us that even when he wasn't physically at work, his mind was there. Like the early Googlers, Rennels simply couldn't turn it off. But, he says, "That all changed when I got serious about mindfulness."

Three years into his work as a consultant, Rennels stumbled upon a few articles and a book about mindfulness meditation. He started studying the practice, and, much like Tan at Google, he saw in mindfulness a solution to many of his problems. He committed to meditating regularly, starting with 1-minute sessions every day.

After just a few weeks, Rennels noticed profound changes. He became more aware of himself and his emotions, and more cognizant of how those emotions precipitated certain actions. His mind still raced at work and when he was actively problem-solving, but he was able to quiet it at the end of the day. He listened better, and he slept better, too. Rennels told us that as he ramped up the duration and frequency of his meditation sessions, he began to feel more in control of himself and no longer at the behest of the world around him. "It was as if every element of my life improved," he recalls.

"TURNING IT OFF": FROM STRESS INTO REST

Mindfulness is about being completely present in the moment, fully aware of yourself and your surroundings. It's helpful to think of the meditation part as highly specific training for being more present at all times of your life. When you meditate, you are strengthening your mindful muscle. It's a simple practice:

- Sit in a comfortable position, ideally in a quiet space.

- Breathe deeply for a few breaths, in and out through your nose.

- Allow your breath to settle back into its natural rhythm and focus on only the sensations of breathing, noticing the rise and fall of your abdomen with each breath; if thoughts arise, notice them, but then direct your focus back to the rhythm and sensation of your breath.

- Set a timer so you don't have to think about time. Start with just 1 minute and gradually increase the duration.

More recently, brain studies are beginning to show the immense and measurable benefits of mindfulness meditation. Researchers are finding that starting at just a few minutes every day, mindfulness meditation increases gray matter in the part of the brain called the prefrontal cortex. The prefrontal cortex is one of the most evolved parts of our brains; its complexity separates us from more primitive animals. In addition to performing higher-order thinking, the prefrontal cortex serves as the brain's command and control center. It allows us to respond thoughtfully to situations instead of instinctively reacting. Having a well-developed prefrontal cortex is especially important when it comes to transitioning out of stress and into rest.

When we challenge ourselves—whether by running a hard workout, learning how to play a new instrument, or working tirelessly to solve a complex problem—we are triggering a stress response in the brain. By strengthening our prefrontal cortex, mindfulness allows us to recognize that we are having a stress response rather than automatically being overcome by it. It's as if we are viewing our thoughts and feelings as a neutral observer and then *choosing* what to do next. A weak prefrontal cortex gets overpowered by a strong stress response. But a strong prefrontal cortex lets us *choose* how we want to respond to stress.

To better understand how this works, researchers at the University of Wisconsin–Madison designed an experiment that allowed them to observe, both inside and out (more on this in a second), the difference between how novice and expert meditators responded to stress. The researchers began by burning the legs of both groups with a scalding-hot wire. At first, both groups responded the same way: with an immediate stress response—"Ouch!" But that was about the only thing the two groups had in common. In addition to watching the participants' outward responses, the researchers were also watching how things unfolded internally, using fMRI scans that let them see inside the participants' brains. What they saw on the inside mirrored exactly what they saw on the outside. At first, the brain region associated with the initial response to stress (the secondary somatosensory cortex) showed the same level of activity in both groups. This represented the earlier "Ouch!"

As the stress response continued, there was noticeable activity in the amygdala of the novice group. The amygdala is one of the less evolved structures in our brain. We share it in common with even the most primitive animals, like rodents. Often referred to as the "emotional center" of the brain, the amygdala controls our most basic instincts, such as hunger and fear. When we sense a threat, it's the amygdala that triggers our stress response: We become tense and brace ourselves for action. While this may be helpful for evading predators in the wild, it's not optimal for keeping our cool when faced with modern-day stressors. The activity in the novices' amygdalas, as evidenced by the fMRI, shed light on why they continued to struggle with pain and discomfort. Their brains were experiencing what neuroscientists call amygdala hijack—an emotional takeover of the brain. They simply couldn't turn off their stress response. Even after the scalding-hot wire was removed, the novices remained in a stressed-out and emotional state.

The expert meditators, on the other hand, demonstrated an entirely different reaction, both inside and out. After the initial burn, they were able to "turn off" their stress response, disassociating the stimulus from an extended emotional reaction. It was as if they felt the pain, thought, "Ouch, that hurts," and then consciously *chose* not to react any further. There was no amygdala hijack inside the brains of the expert meditators. They were able to overcome their innate stress response. This is an extreme example of the same ability that allows the SIYLI mindfulness teacher Brandon Rennels to turn it off at the end of a hard day.

It just so happens that experienced meditators aren't the only experts who can actively choose how to respond to stress. The elite runners that Steve coaches can, too. It's another example of how achieving excellence in seemingly distinct pursuits—running and meditating—ends up having a lot in common.

WHEN PAIN SETS IN during a hard, long workout, everyday runners, and even pretty good ones, often get wrapped up in it. They think to themselves, "Oh crap, this already hurts so much and I've got a long way to go." These emotionally charged thoughts can lead to panic. Heart rates rise and muscles tense. As a result, both enjoyment and performance diminish. But for the best runners, like the ones that Steve

> *It's not that elite runners don't feel pain and discomfort during their hard workouts, it's just that they react differently.*

coaches, it's a different story. It's not that elite runners don't feel pain and discomfort during their hard workouts, it's just that they react differently. Rather than panicking, they have in their minds what Steve calls a "calm conversation."

The calm conversation goes something like this: "This is starting to hurt now. It should. I'm running hard. But I am separate from this pain. It is going to be okay." Just like the expert meditators, Steve's best runners *choose* how they respond to the stress of a workout. Their amygdalas are not hijacked. Although not all of Steve's elite runners meditate, they've all developed a strong mindful muscle through the years of deep, solitary focus that being an elite runner demands. Steve hasn't scanned their brains, but we'd wager that if he did, he'd find their prefrontal cortexes are bursting with gray matter.

On his journey to becoming an elite runner, one of Steve's athletes, Brian Barraza, experienced what numerous young runners do in their first big-time race: failure. When Barraza was a freshman at the University of Houston, he had a chance (and the fitness) to qualify for the 10-K national championship. But instead of finishing in the top 10 like he had all year, Barraza finished a disappointing 28th. Following the race, Barraza told Steve: "That hurt a lot, I just could never get comfortable."

Steve spent a year working with Barraza helping him learn how to become comfortable with being uncomfortable. In particular, he taught Barraza to accept that every hard workout or race was going to hurt. Rather than resisting the pain, Steve taught Barraza to have a calm conversation. Fast-forward a year later to the same race, and, as a sophomore, Barraza took home fourth place, clinching a spot at the national championship. This time around, not only was Barraza's finishing place different, but so, too, was his post-race report: "When it started to hurt, I imagined you were next to me, just like in practice," Barraza told Steve. "It was like I was having a simple conversation in the middle of the race—first with you, then with myself. When it started to get really difficult, I didn't try to force my way through the pain or fight against it. Instead, I reminded myself this is normal and I relaxed."

As a junior, Barraza ran out of his mind and won the qualifying meet. No doubt, his physical fitness certainly improved over the course of his collegiate career. But it was the improvement in his mental fitness that allowed him to fully express it.

Being mindful doesn't just

The calm conversation goes something like this: "This is starting to hurt now. It should. I'm running hard. But I am separate from this pain. It is going to be okay."

help the best athletes get through hard workouts, it also helps them recover. We need look no further than heart rate variability (HRV), or the space between heart beats, for proof. HRV is

> *The adage that hard work separates the best from the rest only explains part of the picture. The best rest harder, too.*

commonly used as a global indicator of physiological recovery. The faster someone's HRV returns to its pre-exercise value (baseline), the better. Research shows that following hard training, the HRV of elite athletes returns to baseline far faster than the HRV of nonelites. In one study, 15 minutes after strenuous exercise the HRV of elite athletes had already returned to 80 percent of its baseline value. The HRV of nonelites, however, was at just 25 percent. After 30 minutes, the HRV of elite athletes had returned to normal, whereas the HRV of nonelites remained at only 40 to 45 percent. Much like the elite meditators, the elite athletes were able to transition from stress to rest much faster than their more novice peers. Perhaps the adage that hard work separates the best from the rest only explains part of the picture. The best rest harder, too.

DEVELOPING YOUR MINDFUL MUSCLE creates space for you to choose how you want to respond to stress. In the middle of a challenge, mindfulness helps you remain calm and collected. It lets you devote all your physical and psychological energy to completing the task at hand, not to worrying about it. After a challenge, mindfulness lets you *choose* to turn off stress and transition to a more restful state. As we've seen, this might mean slowing your racing mind, or slowing your racing heartbeat. Whether you are an engineer or an athlete, mindfulness serves as a gateway to rest, helping you get there faster and more predictably. But as we're about to discover, in an interesting twist, when you enter into that restful state, "rest" turns out to be anything but passive.

PERFORMANCE PRACTICES

- Grow your mindful muscle. The best way to do so is by practicing mindfulness meditation:

  ✓ Choose a time when other distractions are minimized, such as first thing in the morning, after brushing your teeth, or before going to bed.

  ✓ Sit in a comfortable position, ideally in a quiet space.

  ✓ Set a timer so you aren't distracted by thoughts about the passage of time.

  ✓ Begin breathing deeply, in and out through your nose.

  ✓ Allow your breath to settle back into its natural rhythm and focus on nothing but the sensation of breathing, noticing the rise and fall of your abdomen with each breath; if thoughts arise, notice them, but then let them go. Direct your focus back to the sensation of the breath.

  ✓ Start with just 1 minute and gradually increase duration, adding 30 to 45 seconds every few days.

- Frequency trumps duration. It's best to meditate daily, even if that means keeping individual sessions short.

- Apply your growing mindfulness abilities in everyday life.

- Have "calm conversations" during stressful periods.

- Realize when you want to "turn it off" and then *choose* to leave stress behind. Pausing to take a few deep breaths helps to activate the prefrontal cortex, your brain's command and control center.

OUR BRAIN AT REST: THE DEFAULT-MODE NETWORK

In 1929, a German psychiatrist named Hans Berger was conducting a series of studies using a new technology he had invented just 5 years prior.

The technology was called electroencephalogram (or EEG for short) and it mapped electrical activity in the brain. By attaching sensors to the scalps of his patients, Berger could acquire an inside look at their brains. His objective for using this device was to understand which parts of the brain performed different tasks. He asked patients to answer arithmetic questions, instructed them to draw, or had them solve puzzles—all while he monitored the electrical activity in their brains. Sure enough, he saw that different patterns of electrical activity occurred with different types of tasks. Berger and his EEG gave us a whole new insight into how the brain works . . . and also into how the brain doesn't work.

During one of his experiments, Berger left the EEG machine on while a patient was resting between tasks. He noticed that the EEG needles, responsible for tracing electrical activity in the brain, didn't stop moving. Rather, they continued to buzz frenetically. At the time, prevailing wisdom held that the brain essentially turned off when not performing a concrete task. But here was Berger, watching his patients' brains remain extremely active even when they weren't actively doing anything.

When Berger published his findings, the part about the brain being active at rest was largely ignored. Although Berger was quite intrigued by what was happening when his patients *weren't* actively working, the rest of the scientific community was far more concerned with what was happening when they were.

For the next 70 years, research focused on the task-positive network, or the network in the brain that is activated when we perform effortful, attention-demanding tasks. It wasn't until 2001 that Marcus Raichle, MD, a neurologist at Washington University in St. Louis, re-engaged with the puzzling passive activity that Berger had discovered a lifetime ago. Using fMRI scans to look inside the brain, Raichle found that when people zone out and daydream, a particular part of the brain consistently became active. He called this the default-mode network. Interestingly, as soon as Raichle's subjects started focusing again, the default-mode network went black and the task-positive network became active again.

Thanks to the help of more illuminating fMRI technology, unlike

Berger's discovery from almost a century ago, Raichle's work prompted more scientific inquiry on the brain at rest. This body of research shows that even when it feels like our brains are "off," a powerful system, the default-mode network, is running in the background, completely unnoticed by our conscious awareness. And as we're about to see, it's this system—one that is "on" when we are "off"—that is often responsible for creative insight and breakthrough.

EUREKA! HOW TO USHER IN CREATIVITY

Reflect on the times when you are most creative. What are you doing when the answers to tough problems you've been grappling with suddenly pop into your head? Odds are, you aren't trying to solve them. It's more likely that you're zoning out in the shower. If so, you'd be in the company of Woody Allen. Allen relies on the shower for creative spark. He says whenever he is at an impasse, "What will help me is to go upstairs and take a shower . . . So I'll take off some of my clothes and make myself an English muffin or something and try to give myself a little chill so I want to get in the shower." When it comes to generating creative thoughts in the shower, Allen isn't alone, as evidenced by an entire industry of waterproof whiteboards and notebooks.

If not in the shower, maybe your best ideas come to you when you are on a run or a walk. Many esteemed philosophers, from Kierkegaard to Thoreau, held their daily walk as something sacred, the key to generating new ideas. "Methinks that the moment my legs begin to move, my thoughts begin to flow," Thoreau famously penned in his journal.

Or perhaps your epiphany comes when you wake up to use the bathroom in the middle of the night, or when you first emerge from a nap. The best inventors often sleep with a notebook on their nightstands. Thomas Edison was an enthusiastic proponent of power naps. Not because they helped him catch up on sleep, but because he'd awake from them with new ideas.

Lin Manuel Miranda, MacArthur Fellowship "genius grant" winner and creator of the blockbuster Broadway musical *Hamilton*, puts it like this: "A good idea doesn't come when you're doing a million things. The good idea comes in the moment of rest. It comes in the shower. It comes when you're doodling or playing trains with your son. It's when your mind is on the other side of things."

Piece these interesting anecdotes together and a powerful theme emerges. Our most profound ideas often come from the small spaces in between otherwise deliberate thinking: when our brains are at rest. Science bears this out. Researchers have found that despite spending the vast majority of our waking hours in effortful thought, over 40 percent of our creative ideas manifest during breaks.

Most creative discoveries adhere to a standard arc. First, we throw ourselves into the work, intensely deliberating on a topic. While our conscious mind gets us pretty far, every so often there is a missing piece we just can't figure out no matter how hard we try. When we reach this point, though it seems counterintuitive, the best thing we can do is stop trying. Often, if we step away from intentional and active thinking and let our minds rest instead, the missing piece mysteriously appears. Just like the wily veteran runner

> *Our most profound ideas, it seems, tend to come from the small spaces in between otherwise deliberate thinking: when our brains are at rest.*

Deena Kastor (whom you met in Chapter 1) said the magic of her success lies in stepping away from her physical training, the magic of generating creative ideas lies in stepping away from effortful thinking. In order to better understand this magic, we must turn to the difference between the conscious and subconscious minds.

OUR CREATIVE BRAIN

When we are actively working on something, our conscious mind (the task-positive network) runs the show. It functions in a linear and logical "if-then" fashion: if this, then that; if not this, then probably not that. In the vast majority of activities, this sort of linear thinking serves us well. But every once in a while, we get stuck. We may sit and stare at the computer screen or the whiteboard trying to figure something out, but so long as we're still *trying*, we're likely to fail. It's only when we stop trying that our conscious mind fades into the background and our subconscious mind (the default-mode network) takes over.

Our subconscious mind functions in an entirely different manner than our conscious mind. It breaks from the pattern of linear thinking and works much more randomly, pulling information from parts of our brain that are inaccessible when we're consciously working on something. It is in these parts of the brain, in the vast forests bordering the narrow "if-then" highway that our conscious mind runs on, where our creative ideas lie.

It's only when we turn off the conscious mind, shifting into "rest," that insights from the subconscious mind surface.

Neuroscientists have found that the subconscious mind is always working, dully running in the background. But like Raichle discovered, it's only when we turn off the conscious mind, shifting into a state of rest, that insights from the subconscious mind surface.

A mathematician named David Goss, PhD, has firsthand experience with the phenomenon of creativity emerging during periods of rest. Goss is professor emeritus of mathematics at Ohio State University and is internationally recognized for his groundbreaking work in number theory. He's spent the past 40 years creating an entirely new mathematical language in which we can solve problems that cannot be solved in traditional language. In effect, he created a parallel universe for making impossible math problems possible. In order to access the creative insights that led him to develop this parallel universe in math, Goss had to access a parallel universe in his mind.

Goss's love for numbers goes back as far as he can remember. In the early 1970s, when Goss was a freshman at the University of Michigan, he threw himself fully into math. Math, he told us, was all he could think about. Although his performance in math classes was extraordinary, it came at the expense of everything else; he neglected all course work outside of math. During his junior year it got so bad that his advisor told him he needed to shape up or ship out. Goss chose the latter, setting sail for Harvard, where he was welcomed with open arms into a mathematics PhD program. He told us, "I've got a master's and PhD from Harvard, but no undergraduate degree. Oh well."

Relieved of the need to fake it in other disciplines, Goss went on a tear in math. When he was 23 years old, it struck Goss that math was bounded by its current structures. "I remember thinking, there's got to be a better way, a means to advance math beyond what we think is possible," Goss says. This idea, and many of the groundbreaking ones that would follow, didn't come to him at the chalkboard. Rather, he says, "All these crazy ideas came to me via my subconscious. When I was on the exercise bike or just walking around. Some of these ideas were, in fact, crazy. But others turned out to be not so crazy at all." He'd dispose of the crazy ideas the next day. But the not so crazy ones? They turned into a second language for math.

There is no doubt about it, Goss has a brilliant conscious mind. But it's his subconscious mind, and his courage to step away from work and rest so that he can tap into it, that deserves equal celebration. "The subconscious is a crazily powerful thing," Goss told us. "It's almost like the sole reason you do the work is to set the stage for what happens when you step away."

> "The subconscious is a crazily powerful thing," Goss told us. "It's almost like the sole reason you do the work is to set the stage for what happens when you step away."

Although Goss was never a serious athlete, he was following the art of periodization: stressing his mind and then letting it recover only to find new ideas, to grow. Goss isn't the only game-changer who experienced unprecedented success when he stepped away. Next, we'll turn to the story of another great performer, this time a serious athlete, whose courage to rest yielded a different kind of breakthrough. It's the story of a runner named Roger Bannister.

PERFORMANCE PRACTICES

- When you are working on a strenuous mental task and hit an impasse, stop working.
- Step away from whatever it is you are doing for at least 5 minutes.
- The more stressful the task, the longer your break should be.
- For really draining tasks, consider stepping away until the next morning.
- During your breaks, if you aren't sleeping (more on this soon), perform activities that demand little to no effortful thinking. Though we'll explore in great detail how to fill your breaks in Chapter 5, some examples include:

  - ✓ Listening to music
  - ✓ Going on a short walk
  - ✓ Sitting in nature
  - ✓ Taking a shower
  - ✓ Doing the dishes

- You may have an "aha" moment of insight during your break. If you do, great. Even if you don't have an "aha" moment during your break, your subconscious mind is still at work. When you return to whatever it is you were doing, you'll be more likely to make progress.

BREAKTHROUGH

May 6, 1954. Oxford, England. *Bang!* With the firing of the starter's gun, in front of a jam-packed stadium, British track star Roger Bannister started his assault on the impossible: running a mile in under 4 minutes.

In the 1940s and 1950s, the mile, like the marathon of today, was running's most prestigious event. In the same way that today's running community can't stop talking about the possibility of a sub-2-hour marathon, yesteryear's running community was obsessed with the quest for a sub-4-minute mile. The record had been progressively lowered from 4 minutes and 14 seconds (1913) to 4 minutes and 6 seconds (1934) to 4 minutes and 1 second (1945). But there, a single snap of the fingers away from the epic sub-4-minute mile, the record stood for almost a decade. This wasn't for lack of trying. The best runners from all over the world declared they would run sub-4. Their training was designed specifically to break the barrier. But, without fail, they all came up short: 4:03, 4:01, 4:04, 4:02. No one, it seemed, could shave off that final couple of seconds. Physiologists and physicians began to doubt a sub-4 mile was even possible. Man's heart and lungs could not withstand the demands, they reasoned.

Like all the other great runners of the time, Bannister had come close enough, within mere seconds, to think he could break the barrier. So when he declared, in early 1954, that he'd go for the record again, Bannister truly believed he'd get it. But before taking on history, Bannister made what seemed like a very questionable decision. He abandoned his training plan of intense intervals on the track and instead drove off to the mountains of Scotland, only a mere 2 weeks before the race. For days, he and a few buddies didn't speak of, let alone see, a track. Instead, they hiked and climbed in the mountains. They completely checked out of running psychologically and, to a great extent, physically. While hiking is a great activity for developing general fitness, it's a far cry from the blistering 400-meter repeats that Bannister was accustomed to running on the track. In other words, relative to his normal routine, Bannister was resting.

Upon returning to England, Bannister once again shocked everyone in the running community. Instead of immediately hopping on a track in a fit of compulsion to do some "panic training" in the hopes of making up for lost time, he continued to rest. For 3 more days, Bannister let his body recuperate from the demands of the training he'd put in during the months prior. With just a couple days to go before the record attempt, Bannister completed a few short workouts to tune his body up, but that was it. Bannister was physically fresh, and this was a good thing. He would need every last bit of energy to redefine what was possible in running.

Back on the track in Oxford on May 6, 1954. With only one runner nearby, Bannister came through the third lap in 3 minutes and 0.7 seconds, slightly off the sub-4 pace. *Ding!* When the bell rang signifying the final lap, Bannister burst into a maddening drive. As he slowly pulled away from the field, everyone in the crowd rose to their feet: 3:40, 3:41, 3:42. . . . Down the final straightaway, the energy was palpable, fans screaming at the top of their lungs . . . 3:54, 3:55. . . . As Bannister crossed the finish line, unaware of anything other than how hard he was pushing himself, the crowd roared. The stadium announcer, Norris McWhirter, who would go on to found the Guinness World Records, burst onto the loudspeaker with his most memorable call:

> *Ladies and gentlemen, here is the result of event nine, the one mile: first, number 41, R.G. Bannister, Amateur Athletic Association and formerly of Exeter and Merton Colleges, Oxford, with a time which is a new meeting and track record, and which— subject to ratification—will be a new English native, British national, all-comers, European, British Empire and world record. The time was three . . .*

The crowd erupted and the rest of the announcement faded into oblivion. In 3 minutes, 59 and 4/10 of a second, Roger Bannister had broken one of the greatest barriers in human history. And it was in no small part due to his courage to rest.

ALTHOUGH BANNISTER'S ESCAPE TO the woods is a bit extreme, the notion of taking breaks to facilitate physical growth is anything but that. We asked Matt Dixon, a preeminent coach of the world's top triathletes, what separates the best from the rest. The answer, he told us, is the rest. Sure, it takes a sage like Dixon to effectively balance training across triathlon's three disciplines (swim, bike, run), but Dixon's real magic is how he convinces his athletes to rest.

No different than professionals in any other highly demanding industry, triathletes are eager to push. They see their competition putting in endless hours of training and feel like there is always something more they could be doing. Unlike in pure running, where athletes often show restraint for fear of broken bones, triathlon includes the nonimpact sports of swimming and cycling. In these sports, athletes see little reason to hold themselves back, and many don't. As a result, triathletes, perhaps more than any other type of athlete, suffer from overtraining syndrome and burnout. But not so with Dixon's athletes.

Dixon tells us, somewhat reluctantly, that he has become known as the "recovery coach." This is in no small part because so many overtrained athletes, beaten down and on the brink of burnout, turn to Dixon to save their careers. Dixon says that the hardest part of getting athletes to rest is convincing them that doing so will benefit them more than additional training. Once they make that jump, he says, then it's easy: "The athletes start gaining more fitness and performing better than ever before." For the first time in their careers, he told us, "They are giving their bodies time and space to adapt to the training stress."

> By framing rest as something that supports growth and adaption, Dixon's athletes stop viewing rest as passive, as "not training." And just like that, rest becomes as productive as an additional workout.

In order to help his athletes make this crucial jump, Dixon frames rest as an active choice.* When Dixon writes training plans for Ironman triathletes, there are no "easy" or "off" days. There are, however, plenty of "supporting sessions." By framing rest as something that supports growth and adaption, Dixon's athletes stop viewing rest as passive, as "not training." And just like that, rest becomes as productive as an additional workout. This simple shift in mindset enables Dixon to do what so few coaches can: convince his athletes to rest. Like Bannister, Dixon's athletes show up to

---

* Dixon is taking advantage of something behavioral scientists call the commission bias, or our innate preference for action over inaction.

big races not just fitter but also fresher than their competitors. They win major races not because they train harder than their competitors, but because they rest harder than their competitors.

IN A SOCIETY THAT glorifies grinding, short-term gains and pushing to extremes, it takes guts to rest. Just as Dixon does with the triathletes he coaches, perhaps we should all reframe rest. Rest isn't lazily slothing around; it's an active process in which physical and psychological growth occurs. To reap the benefits of stress, you need to rest.

In the next chapter, we turn to the question of what, exactly, is the best way to rest. We'll present the science behind rest breaks of various durations—from short pauses throughout the day to the critical importance of sleep to extended vacations—and explain how you can strategically maximize the unique benefits of each type. It is our hope that when you see how practical and powerful these breaks can be, you'll feel better about actively choosing to take them.

5

REST LIKE THE BEST

In Chapter 3, we discussed the benefits of athletics-style interval training in pursuits far beyond athletics. We also touched upon a large body of research demonstrating how, regardless of the task at hand, our output begins to suffer after 2 consecutive hours of hard work. We learned that we do our best work in cycles of intense effort followed by short breaks. In Chapter 4, we explored the practice of mindfulness, and discussed the value of stepping away from our work so as to engage the creative power of our subconscious mind. There are many ways to step away from our work of course, and not all of them are created equal. Browsing social media, for example, isn't nearly as effective as taking a walk.

Let's now turn to the unique benefits of different kinds of breaks, supported by the stories of great performers and the latest science. We'll start by considering short breaks that you can use throughout the day, and we'll end by examining the value (and challenge) of extended periods of rest. Think of what follows as a menu of "rest" options from which you can strategically choose.

WALKING BREAKS

In his book *The War of Art*, award-winning author Steven Pressfield writes of his walks: "I take a pocket tape recorder because I know that as my surface mind empties with the walk, another part of me will chime in and start talking . . . The word 'leer' on page 342 should be 'ogle' instead; You repeated yourself in Chapter 21. The last sentence is just like the one in the middle of Chapter 7." As you learned in the previous chapter, Pressfield is not alone. Many of the best writers and thinkers have sworn by their walking breaks.

Taking a stroll isn't just useful for creatives like writers, artists, and inventors. When Brad was working on complicated financial models at McKinsey & Company, he'd take walks throughout the day, especially when he felt stuck. Almost without fail, what he couldn't figure out while staring at the screen popped into his mind during or immediately following a walk.

Stepping away from your work takes a lot of guts, especially when you're on a tight deadline. Sometimes you simply don't have the time to walk very far. The good news is that even short walks can provide big benefits.

In a study cleverly titled *Give Your Ideas Some Legs: The Positive Effect of Walking on Creative Thinking*, researchers from Stanford University examined the effects of a short walking break. They instructed subjects to take short walking breaks outdoors, indoors, or not at all. Following their walk, they assessed participants' creativity. They asked them to generate as many nontraditional uses as possible for common items. For example, a tire could be used as a floatation device, as a basketball hoop, or as a swing. (This is called a Guilford's Alternate Uses Test and is a commonly used method for measuring creativity.) Those who took as brief as a 6-minute walk outdoors increased creativity by more than 60 percent versus those who had remained seated at their desks. Although walking outdoors yielded the most pronounced benefits, those who walked indoors still generated about 40 percent more cre-

Even short walks can provide big benefits.

ative ideas than those who didn't walk at all. This suggests that even if you can't walk outside (e.g., it's winter, there are no sidewalks nearby, etc.), taking a few laps around the office or hopping on a treadmill is still highly beneficial.

At first, the researchers suspected that increased bloodflow to the brain was the culprit behind the walks' benefits. However, it appears that the benefits might also stem from the interplay between walking and attention. Since walking requires just enough coordination to occupy the part of our brain responsible for effortful thinking, it ever so slightly distracts our conscious mind. As a result, when walking, it's easier to tap into our creative engine, our subconscious. This explains why walking tends to be more effective at fostering creativity than other movements that require greater focus and coordination, like dancing or lifting weights. Walking occupies us just

> *Walking is the perfect gateway into the subconscious mind and for stimulating creative insight that can help us overcome mental gridlock.*

enough to help us stop thinking about whatever it is we were working on, but not too much as to prevent mind-wandering. It's the perfect gateway into the subconscious mind and for stimulating creative insight that can help us overcome mental gridlock.

In addition to the cognitive benefits, walking breaks are also great for physical health. You've probably heard by now that "sitting is the new smoking." Long, uninterrupted bouts of sitting are awful for your health, and sitting can even undo gains from exercise. Fortunately, the latest science shows that taking just a 2-minute walk every hour is protective against many of sitting's ill effects. One study showed that these short walks reduce the risk of premature death (i.e., "all-cause mortality," or any cause of death) by 33 percent. In ancient Greece, when Athenian culture was flourishing and at its peak, Plato and his contemporaries didn't separate physical from intellectual education and development. These wise philosophers were on to something that we are now rediscovering: Sound mind and sound body go hand in hand.

ALL NATURAL

In 2008, a University of Michigan psychologist named Marc Berman, PhD, sought to explore why so many great creators, from DaVinci to Darwin, reported being inspired by nature. To test whether there is truly a strong connection between nature and creativity, Berman enlisted undergraduate students and divided them into two groups. Both groups went through the same initial series of rigorous cognitive tasks. After finishing, one of the groups took a break in a secluded park while the other group took a break in a busy urban setting. On a subsequent series of challenging cognitive tasks, the students who took a break in a natural setting outperformed those who took their break in an urban setting.

Perhaps you're thinking: "Okay, but accessing a secluded park in the middle of the day isn't so easy." Worry not—simply looking at pictures of nature can help. In a second experiment, Berman had students go through the same process just described, only this time, rather than go outside, they were instructed to view pictures (for just 6 minutes) of either natural or urban areas. The result was the same: The students who viewed pictures of nature significantly outperformed their urban-viewing counterparts.

Berman hypothesizes that nature inherently makes us feel good and improves our mood, thereby hastening our transition from the stress of hard work to a more restful state and promoting mind-wandering and subsequent creativity. Even if all you can manage is switching windows on your computer, try browsing a *National Geographic* or *Outside* magazine story with pictures of nature rather than your Facebook or Twitter feed.

Exposure to nature not only helps with creativity, but it may also lower levels of Interleukin-6 (IL-6), a molecule associated with inflammation in the body. Lower levels of IL-6 can prevent the harmful, chronic type of inflammation that often sidelines serious athletes. According to a study published in the journal *Emotion*, more than any other positive feeling, awe, an emotion commonly brought about by nature, is linked to lower levels of IL-6. We asked the lead author of the study, Jennifer Stellar, PhD, what might be going on here. How can something as simple as being in nature, or even just looking at pictures of nature, change our biology?

Stellar told us that "experiencing awe makes us feel more connected to the universe and more humble." These feelings, she says, "probably help to 'switch off' our stress response, in turn lessening inflammation."

After your next hard workout or stressful day at the office, consider sitting in a park before you rush into an ice bath, pop anti-inflammatory drugs, or take the latest and greatest relaxation supplement. As Cheryl Strayed's mother said in the popular book and movie *Wild*, when you are feeling down, "Put yourself in the way of beauty."

MEDITATION

Earlier we discussed how mindfulness meditation, the practice of sitting and focusing on only your breath, can help hasten the transition from stress to rest. Mindfulness meditation strengthens the prefrontal cortex, which is the part of your brain that lets you *choose* how to respond to stress. Thus, we recommend a daily meditation practice to train your mindful muscle. In addition, unplanned, on-the-spot meditation can also be valuable during short breaks from physically or mentally taxing work.

Whether you are tense because you are cranking out a memo on a tight deadline or because you are cranking out heavy sets in the weight room, mindfulness meditation can help improve your performance. The feeling of being wound up is the physiological manifestation of the mind bracing for a threat, and it enters into stress mode. If you remain stressed after taking a break (by stepping away from the keyboard or the barbell), you will lose much of the break's effectiveness. It's not hard to tell if your break is being hijacked by lingering stress. You generally feel it in your shoulders (are they raised?), forearms (are they flexed?), and jaw (is it clenched?). If you experience these sensations, you might want to consider a short bout of mindfulness meditation. Sit down in a comfortable position, close your eyes, and take 10 deep breaths, in and out through your nose. Focus on only the sensation of your breath. Physical pain, tightness, and negative thoughts may arise. If they do, do not ignore them. Rather, acknowledge them non-judgmentally, let them go, and then return to focusing on your breath.

After you've taken 10 breaths, you could continue focusing exclusively on your breath for the duration of your break. Or, you could consider transitioning to a technique called "open-monitoring" meditation, sometimes referred to as a "body scan." In open-monitoring meditation, though you continue to breathe rhythmically, you shift your focus from your breath to various parts of your body. Start at your feet and work your way up. Focus on the feeling of your toes in your shoes, your skin against a chair (or your clothes), your muscles loosening, and your heart beating. Studies show that just 7 to 10 minutes of open-monitoring meditation aids in both physiological recovery and creativity.*

> *Whether you are tense because you are cranking out a memo on a tight deadline or because you are cranking out heavy sets in the weight room, mindfulness meditation can help improve your performance.*

SOCIAL RECOVERY

One of us (Steve) has tried numerous ways of expediting recovery in the athletes he coaches after intense training sessions, but by far the most effective is social interaction. That's right—Steve's secret isn't massage, compression, or cryotherapy. It's cultivating fun and laid-back environments where his athletes can hang out with each other. Following competitions or especially challenging practices, Steve more or less mandates his athletes attend team breakfasts, lunches, or movie/game nights. Fascinating new science backs him up.

The ratio of the hormones testosterone to cortisol acts as a good indicator of systemic recovery (the higher this ratio, the better). A study out of Bangor University in the UK found this ratio was higher in athletes who went through their post-game analysis in a social environment with friends

---

* It's worth reiterating that open-monitoring is different from sitting mindfulness meditation, which focuses on only the breath. While the former is great for short breaks, it should not replace the latter. Mindfulness meditation is powerful as a daily practice that allows you to choose how to respond to stress throughout the day, every day. That's why we recommended incorporating sitting mindfulness meditation into your daily life, irrespective of breaks.

than in athletes who went through it in a neutral environment with strangers. What's more is that the group in the social environment actually performed better in competition a week later. The lead author on this study, Christian Cook, PhD, professor of physiology and elite performance at Bangor University, told us that "a friendly post-exercise setting—particularly being able to talk, joke, and debrief with other athletes—seems to help with recovery and future performance."

When we shared this with Kelly McGonigal, PhD, (the Stanford University professor and stress expert you met in Chapter 3), she wasn't surprised. "The basic biology of feeling connected to others has profound effects on stress physiology," McGonigal told us. The positive effects of social connection include increasing heart rate variability (HRV), shifting the nervous system into recovery mode, and releasing hormones such as oxytocin and vasopressin that

> "The basic biology of feeling connected to others has profound effects on stress physiology. . . . It's pretty poetic that feeling connected to others literally fixes a broken heart."

have anti-inflammatory and antioxidant properties. "What's even crazier," says McGonigal, "is that oxytocin helps your heart repair. It's pretty poetic that feeling connected to others literally fixes a broken heart."

Although you can use social recovery throughout the day, it's only effective if the environment is relaxed. Going to coffee with a colleague only to discuss work won't do you much good. That's why we recommend this strategy for the end of your workday. But that doesn't mean it's easy. When we are feeling stressed, often our natural inclination is to retreat inward and wall ourselves off from the outside world. In the worst cases, the stress lingers and grows and we put ourselves at risk for a vicious cycle of rumination: Just ask an athlete who finished an intense training session and isn't feeling so good about it; an artist who got nothing done at the studio; or a businessperson who had a rough day at the office. Even though we may not always want to be sociable, the benefits of surrounding ourselves with friends and kicking back are enormous, *especially* following demanding situations.

PERFORMANCE PRACTICES

- Have the courage to takes breaks throughout the day, *especially* when you are stuck or feeling unbearable stress; the more intense the work, the more frequent the breaks.

- Take a walk lasting at least 6 minutes to increase creativity and decrease the ill effects of sitting. If you can, walk outdoors, but even taking a few laps around the office provides big benefits.

- Put yourself in the way of beauty. Being in nature, or even just looking at pictures of nature, helps with the transition from stress to rest and promotes creative thinking.

- Meditate. Begin with a few mindful breaths, focusing only on the breath. Then, consider shifting to open-monitoring meditation, scanning your body and shifting your awareness to all of its sensations.

- Hang out with friends! At the end of hard work—be it with your body or your mind—surrounding yourself with friends in a laid-back environment fundamentally alters your biology from stress to rest.

Yes, that's right, we just provided you with the scientific basis for getting drinks with friends. (Note: We did not say "happy hour." Happy hour tends to be a time when people who work together go out to commiserate about work. As such, far too often these hours are generally not very happy. Go hang out with your friends instead.)

SLEEP

If you often feel tired, and know that you just don't get enough sleep, you have company. Lots of company. About 195 million Americans, to be exact. That's right, a whopping 65 percent of Americans get less than the medically recommended 7 to 9 hours of sleep each night. Forty percent sleep less than 6 hours. This wasn't always the case. In 1942, the average American slept 7.9 hours every night. Today, that number is down to 6.8 hours.

Much, if not all, of our collective sleep loss is related to the technologies that keep us connected at all times and allow us to work at all hours. We feel compelled to be online and pressured to do more and more work. "There just aren't enough hours in the day," we tell ourselves, so we've taken to working in the night. This is particularly true in the business world, where we far too often hear stories venerating CEOs who "need only 4 hours of sleep." (A different story emerges when you ask these CEOs how happy they are with their lives, or when you examine their tenures.) In reality, working immediately prior to bedtime is an awful idea. That's because even if we finish the work at a reasonable hour, the screens we stare at actually keep us up for hours thereafter.

Most digital devices with screens, be it computers, smartphones, iPads, or televisions—in other words, pretty much everything that we peer into in the evening—emit something called blue light. Of all the types of artificial light that mess with sleep, the blue variety is by far the worst. While we can rebound from being in a room where the light bulbs are on, it's much harder to rebound from staring at a screen. Blue light throws our circadian rhythm (the body's natural clock) completely out of whack. Depending on when we are exposed to it, blue light can shift our internal clocks by up to six time zones. This is why when you have a creative idea in the middle of the night, it's best to write it down on a paper notebook and not run to your computer to start working on it. This should also serve as a warning against the increasingly common habit of checking smartphones throughout the night.

In a recent study examining the ill effects of blue light, Harvard researchers had participants read from either a traditional book or a blue light–emitting e-book 4 hours prior to going to bed. After just 5 consecutive days of reading in this manner, the differences between the two groups were stark. Those who read the e-book reported feeling far less sleepy when it was time to go to bed. This feeling was rooted in their biochemistry. Unlike those who read from a traditional book, the e-book readers experienced a 90-minute delay in their bodies' release of melatonin, the hormone that makes us feel sleepy. Although they hadn't traveled across time

We think we are missing out on a lot by sleeping, but in fact we are missing out on far more by not sleeping. Sleep is one of the most productive things we can do.

zones, their bodies' internal clocks thought they had. Their circadian rhythms had shifted dramatically, making it harder for them to fall asleep and making them feel less rested (and more groggy) upon waking up. Most worrisome is that these effects resulted from just 5 days of using a blue light–emitting device 4 *hours* before bedtime. Not to mention, these profound effects came from *reading for pleasure.* You could imagine the results would be far worse if the task was sending emails or working on deadline documents. Blue light alone is detrimental. Combine blue light with a racing mind, and it becomes easier to understand why we're sleeping less than ever.

At the end of this section we are going to recommend that you limit blue light prior to bedtime and provide you with a handful of other tips to get a better night's sleep, but first we are obliged to turn a common notion on its head. We think we are missing out on a lot by sleeping, but in fact we are missing out on far more by not sleeping. Sleep is one of the most productive things we can do. We don't grow when we're in the gym or when we're immersed in our work: We grow in our sleep.

Sleep and Our Growing Mind

We can put in all the work in the world while we're awake, but if we don't sleep, much of its value is lost. Literally. That's because one of sleep's foremost benefits is the role it plays in how we consolidate and store—that is, how we remember—new information. Sleep's critical role in learning is a rather new discovery. Robert Stickgold, MD, PhD, a preeminent sleep researcher at Harvard, told the *New Yorker* magazine that until recently, people thought "the only known function of sleep was to cure sleepiness." That's changed quite a bit since the turn of the century, and in no small part thanks to Stickgold's research.

In 2000, Stickgold published the results of a clever experiment that would forever change how we think about sleep. Stickgold invited three groups of people to immerse themselves in the computer game *Tetris*, playing for 7 hours a day, 3 days straight. One group had played *Tetris* before, another group was familiar with the game, and a third group couldn't remember whether they'd played before—they literally had severe amnesia.

During each of the experiment's 3 nights, the study participants were awoken repeatedly and asked to recall what they'd been dreaming about. Most of the time, the answer was *Tetris*. Even the amnesiacs reported dreaming of *Tetris*. Although they couldn't remember anything about the experiment the following day, the amnesiacs did remember having dreamed of falling shapes and patterns. Stickgold proved that during sleep, on a very deep level we process the experiences and information that we gather while we are awake. When we sleep, and in particular when we dream, the brain goes through the countless things we were exposed to throughout the day—the cars we saw in a parking lot, the story arc of the TV show we watched, the ideas we generated, the new people we met, and so forth—and decides what is worth storing in memory. It also figures out where in our web of knowledge to store these things.

Since Stickgold's foundational study, numerous others have also demonstrated that we assess, consolidate, and retain information in our sleep. We now know that sleep isn't just important for processing intellectual knowledge, but for how we encode emotional experiences, too. In all our conversations with artists, sleep was linked to periods of high creativity and emotional fire. This isn't at all surprising. Research shows that sleep enhances the vividness of how we process and recall emotional events. As a matter of fact, given all of the emotional activity that happens in our sleep, scientists are beginning to wonder if insomnia is not only the result of many mood disorders but also a *cause*. Much like sleep helps us make sense of information, it also helps us make sense of our emotions.

Sleep also impacts our self-control. In a review of numerous studies, researchers from Clemson University found that chronically sleep-deprived

> *There are increasing marginal returns to sleep. Hours 7 to 9—the hours that the majority of us never get—are actually the most powerful.*

individuals have less self-control and are at increased risk for "succumbing to impulsive desires, poor attentional capacity, and compromised decision making." People who don't get enough sleep (7 to 9 hours per night) perform worse on just about anything that requires effort and attention, whether that means solving complex problems, learning a new skill, or sticking to a diet. It's as if sleep not only helps you get the most out of what you did today, but also gives you the energy for the challenges you aspire to take on tomorrow. In the words of Matt Dixon, the triathlon coach who espouses the value of rest, sleep is the most important "supporting session" there is.

Almost all of sleep's benefits occur in the later stages, mainly during something called REM, or rapid eye movement. We spend only about 20 to 25 percent of our total sleep time in REM. And, in an interesting twist, the longer we sleep, the greater the proportion of it is in REM. That's because REM time increases with each sleep cycle. In other words, there are increasing marginal returns to sleep. Hours 7 to 9—the hours that the majority of us never get—are actually the most powerful.

Yet again, "rest" proves to be anything but passive. As one of our favorite science writers, Maria Konnikova, put it in her wonderful *New Yorker* magazine series on sleep,* "As we sleep, our brains replay, process, learn, and extract meaning. In a sense, they think."

Let's pause for just a moment to reflect upon this in the context of the equation stress + rest = growth. During our waking hours we expose ourselves to all kinds of psychological stimulus (stress), and during our sleep (rest) we make sense of it all. As a result, we're

> *In our sleep, we grow. And we grow not just our cognitive and emotional muscles but our physical ones, too.*

---

* Konnikova's three-part series changed the way both of us think about sleep. We highly recommend you read it. See the references on pages 210 and 211 for details.

literally more evolved when we wake up the next morning. In our sleep, we grow. And we grow not just our cognitive and emotional muscles but our physical ones, too.

Sleep and Our Growing Body

Over the past few years, Brad has had the privilege of interviewing more than 40 world-class athletes for a series in *Outside* magazine on the habits of great performers. These individuals include some of the world's best runners, skiers, cyclists, surfers, kayakers, and climbers. To Brad's surprise, he found a fair amount of variability in their daily habits. Some do yoga religiously, others have never stretched before. Some are gluten-free vegans, others make red meat the centerpiece of their diets. Some take ice baths, others favor heat. One topic where there is complete conformity, however, is sleep. The best athletes in the world all prioritize sleep just as much as they prioritize their hardest training sessions and their most important competitions. Three-time Ironman world champion and course record holder Mirinda Carfrae told Brad, "Sleep might be the most important thing I do." She was being serious, and for good reason. According to the latest performance science, most of us could benefit from adopting Carfrae's mindset.

> *The best athletes in the world all prioritize sleep just as much as they prioritize their hardest training sessions and their most important competitions.*

As you learned in Chapter 2, when we stress our bodies, they enter into something called a "catabolic" state. Our muscles, and even our bones, break down on a micro scale. The hormone cortisol is released, telling our body, "Help! We can't handle this stress." We become tired and sore, which is the body's natural way of informing us it's time to take a rest. If we neglect rest and keep pushing, the breakdown continues and, eventually, our health and performance suffer. But if we listen and allow the body to rest, it shifts from a catabolic state to an anabolic one, in which the body repairs and rebuilds so that it can come back stronger. This is to say that the stress of hard physical training breaks us down, and it is only when we follow stress with rest that adaptation and growth occurs. This is especially true with sleeping, which is a catalyst for physical growth. Just as the brain is actively processing the work we've done throughout the day, when we sleep the body is doing the same.

Once we've been sleeping for at least an hour, anabolic hormones start to flood our system. Testosterone and human growth hormone (HGH), both of which are integral to muscle and bone growth, are released after the first REM cycle and stay elevated until we wake. These hormones increase protein synthesis, or the generation of proteins specifically designed to facilitate physical repair.* This means much of the protein athletes eat, diligently counted gram by gram throughout the day, goes to waste if they aren't sleeping enough.

Similar to the benefits of sleep for our brains, the benefits of sleep for our bodies also increase the longer we sleep. This is because with each additional sleep cycle we receive another pulse of powerful anabolic hormones. In other words, you can get more of the same hormones that countless athletes have risked their health, reputations, and careers for (by injecting synthetic steroids, aka doping) simply by sleeping for a few additional hours. Of course, the testosterone and HGH released when you sleep are not synthetic, and they are balanced by other naturally occurring hormones. Unlike illegal steroids, they are great for your health. If you've been searching for the fountain of youth or taking all sorts of crazy supplements, you can stop now. Instead, simply get under the covers and close your eyes.

If you've been searching for the fountain of youth or taking all sorts of crazy supplements, you can stop now. Instead, simply get under the covers and close your eyes.

---

* Studies show that ingesting 20 to 30 grams of protein prior to sleep increases protein synthesis overnight. As such, many elite athletes have taken note and drink a whey- or casein-based protein drink prior to sleeping.

With all these benefits, it's no wonder the best athletes in the world prioritize sleep. It's not that they sleep because they are elite. They are elite because they sleep.

Unfortunately, far too many active people don't follow the example set by the best athletes. Instead, they fall into a trap of thinking that it's better to get in just a bit more training and they sacrifice sleep to do so. This kind of thinking is especially prevalent in very busy people, like amateur athletes (busy with jobs) and student athletes (busy with school). Don't get us wrong: You absolutely need to train hard to get better. Without the stimulus of stress, you can rest all you want and there still won't be growth. But sneaking in that extra hour of training at the expense of sleep is rarely a good idea.

One place that understands the value of sleep for busy athletes is Stanford University. In a 2011 study, players on the varsity basketball team were told to maintain their usual sleep routine for a 2- to 4-week period during which baseline performance data was collected. Measures of performance specific to basketball—things such as sprint speed, shooting accuracy, and reaction time—were recorded after every practice. After the initial baseline period, the players were told to focus on getting as much sleep as possible for the next 6 to 7 weeks. The researchers asked the athletes to strive for a *minimum* of 10 hours, promising they'd see performance benefits. The hoop stars listened: On average, they slept for an additional 1 hour and 50 minutes every night. Following the sleep extension period, the players were retested on all the performance measures. The results were profound. They sprinted 4 percent faster, shot both free throws and three-pointers with 9 percent better accuracy, and demonstrated significantly faster reaction time. Remember, these weren't middle school or even high school kids. These were athletes at a Division I powerhouse. This level of performance enhancement was nothing short of extraordinary. The extra sleep also translated to wins on the court. In 2011 (the year of the study) the Stanford team won 26 games (up from just 15 the previous year) and won the National Invitation Tournament (NIT) title. They followed that with an NCAA Sweet 16 appearance in 2012 and another NIT title in 2014.

To prove this wasn't a fluke, the same researchers replicated the experiment with varsity swimmers. The results were the same. After the period of extended sleep, the swimmers' performance skyrocketed. They sprinted faster, reacted quicker off the blocks, improved turn time, and increased kick-stroke volume. According to the lead author on the studies, Cheri Mah, "Many of the Stanford coaches are definitely more aware of the importance of sleep. Coaches have even started to adjust their practice and traveling schedules to allow for proper sleep habits. For many athletes and coaches, this study was the first time they truly understood how large of an impact sleep can have on their performance and results." If an institution with one of the best combination of athletes and researchers in the entire world says we should sleep more to improve our physical performance, then perhaps we should listen.

Napping

Regardless of what all the "life hackers" may tell you, napping does *not* make up for insufficient nighttime sleep. You can't nap your way to growth, be it physical or psychological. That said, napping does help restore energy and concentration during midday lulls, so it's a strategy worth considering for long and intense days.

A growing body of research demonstrates that naps can improve performance, alertness, concentration, and judgment. Given these attributes are all critical for those on a space station orbiting the earth, it should come as no surprise that NASA became interested in learning about the benefits of napping. When NASA scientists conducted studies on astronauts, they discovered that a 25-minute nap improved judgment by 35 percent and vigilance by 16 percent. No surprise, then, that NASA encourages afternoon snoozes. In another study, and one more relevant to most of our earthly situations, researchers pitted napping against coffee. They found that individuals who took a nap of 15 to 20 minutes awoke with more alertness and went on to perform better during the remainder of the day than those who, instead of napping, drank 150 milligrams of caffeine, or about the same amount in a Starbucks grande-size coffee.

When we take short naps, the part of our brain that is always on when we are awake has the opportunity to take a break. Much like a fatigued muscle rejuvenates during a short breather, so, too, does this part of our brain. In a critical review on the efficacy of napping, sleep scientists found that a 10-minute nap yields the greatest benefits, though most experts say anything under 30 minutes is effective. Even if you don't actually experience the sensation of falling asleep, simply closing your eyes can help switch your active brain off, allowing it to recover. Staying asleep for more than 30 minutes, however, can be counterproductive. This is because with longer naps we run the risk of waking up feeling even groggier and more sluggish than before we fell asleep. This condition, called "sleep inertia," occurs when we are awoken in the middle of a deep sleep cycle. The grogginess is the body and brain's natural way of telling us to go back to sleep so it can finish what it started. (Hence the term "inertia.") Deep sleep generally doesn't begin until after about 30 minutes, which is why experts suggest making that the upper limit for a nap's duration.*

The next time you are fighting to keep your eyes open in the mid-to-late afternoon, experiment with taking a short snooze. Forward-thinking companies like Google and Apple have designated nap rooms. Some of the best thinkers in history, including Albert Einstein and Winston Churchill, were big proponents of the midday nap.

EXTENDED BREAKS

At the end of this year, Bernard Lagat, one of the best American runners ever, will take a break. For 5 weeks, he'll hang up his sneakers and complete little to no exercise. This isn't something new or brought about by old

---

* In certain instances, taking a longer nap of 90 minutes to 2 hours may make sense. Extended naps mimic, for both the brain and the body, what occurs during nighttime sleep. Unfortunately, longer naps can also interfere with nighttime sleep, which is far more important. Therefore, most experts only recommend extended naps for individuals who genuinely need the additional deep sleep during the day, in that it doesn't interfere with their nighttime sleep. Elite athletes completing grueling two-a-day workouts are a good example of a group that could stand to benefit from longer naps. The famed American distance runner Meb Keflezighi says he uses a full arsenal of naps ranging in duration from 15 to 90 minutes.

PERFORMANCE PRACTICES

- Sleep is productive.

- Aim for at least 7 to 9 hours of sleep per night. For those doing intense physical activity, 10 hours is *not* too much.

- The best way to figure out the right amount of sleep for you is to spend 10 to 14 days going to sleep when you are tired and waking up without an alarm clock. Take the average sleep time. That's what you need.

- For a better night's sleep, follow these tips, consolidated from the world's leading researchers:

  ✓ Ensure you expose yourself to natural (i.e., non-electric) light throughout the day. This will help you maintain a healthy circadian rhythm.

  ✓ Exercise. Vigorous physical activity makes us tired. When we are tired, we sleep. But don't exercise too close to bedtime.

  ✓ Limit caffeine intake, and phase it out completely 5 to 6 hours prior to your bedtime.

  ✓ Only use your bed for sleep and sex. Not for eating, watching television, working on your laptop, or anything else. The one exception is reading a paper book prior to bed.

age for this 43-year-old athlete. If anything, part of the reason Lagat, who has run in five Olympics and won two world championships, remains atop the international running scene is *because* of this break, which he's been taking every year since 1999. "Rest," Lagat says, "is a good thing."

Lagat credits his annual respite with keeping him physically and psychologically healthy over the years. The extended shutdown period allows his body to recuperate from grinding 80-mile running weeks. Although Lagat's year-end break might be the longest, nearly all his peers at the top of running take similar ones, ranging from 10 days to 5 weeks. Olympic 1500-meter silver medalist Leo Manzano recently told the *Wall Street Journal* that he, too, needs at least a month to recover from the season. His

✓ Don't drink alcohol close to bedtime. Although alcohol can hasten the onset of sleep, it often disrupts the later and more important stages.

✓ Limit blue light exposure in the evening.

✓ Don't start working on hard, stressful activities—be them mental or physical—after dinner.

✓ If you struggle with a racing mind, try inserting a brief mindfulness meditation session prior to bed.

✓ When you feel yourself getting drowsy, don't fight it. Whatever you are doing can wait until the morning.

✓ Keep your room as dark as possible. If feasible, consider black-out blinds.

✓ Keep your smartphone OUT of the bedroom entirely. Not on silent. Out.

• Try taking a nap of 10 to 30 minutes to help restore energy and focus if you hit a mid-afternoon lull.

reasoning is simple: "It feels like I've been going nonstop since November."

Take a moment and ask yourself: Have you ever felt like Manzano? If so, did you take a month off? Did you even take the weekend off? As we discussed in the Introduction of this book, for the vast majority of Americans the answer to both of those questions is no. We consistently work on weekends and rarely use all our paid time off, let alone take extended vacations. Instead, we get trapped into thinking that if we're not always working hard, we'll be surpassed by the competition. Our misguided thinking is the result of years of conditioning. We (i.e., Brad and Steve) both remember growing up to the tune of popular inspirational quotes like, "When you are not practicing, remember somewhere someone else is, and if you meet him, he will win." Unfortunately, we've lost the notion of *smart* work at the expense of *hard* work, which somehow almost always gets confused with *more* work.

But here's the thing: If we never take "easy" periods, we are never able to go full throttle and the "hard" periods end up being not that hard at all. We get stuck in a gray zone, never really stressing ourselves but never really resting either. This vicious cycle is often referred to by a much less vicious name—"going through the motions"—but it's a huge problem nonetheless. That's because few people grow when they are going through the motions. In order to give it our all, and do so over a long time horizon without burning out, we've got to be more like Bernard Lagat: Every now and then, we've got to take it *really* easy. In addition to his year-end break, Lagat also takes an off-day at the end of every hard training week. On his off-days, Lagat doesn't even think about running. Instead, he engages only in activities that relax and restore both his body and mind such as massage, light stretching, watching his favorite TV shows, drinking wine, and playing with his kids.

If we never take "easy" periods, we are never able to go full throttle and the "hard" periods end up being not that hard at all.

We are not suggesting that you haphazardly take off-days and extended vacations. Rather, in the same spirit that Lagat does, we are recommending that you strategically insert longer periods of rest to follow longer periods of stress. The modern Monday through Friday workweek was, in essence, founded upon that premise. The concept of a "weekend" was devised in the early 1900s to accommodate both the Christian and Jewish Sabbaths, the religious versions of rest days. Today, however, too few of us observe the Sabbath—either religiously or symbolically. Alternatively, we continue working on the same projects we were working on during the week or add additional stressors in other dimensions of our lives. Few of us rest on the weekends.

There is a high cost of neglecting to rest on the weekends: The quality of the work we do during the week suffers, leaving us feeling pressured to work on Saturday and Sunday just to catch up. We get caught in the vicious cycle: not enough stress to demand rest, not enough rest to support real stress. If you are stuck in this cycle right now, try ending it this coming weekend. Give yourself at least one day off, in which you completely disconnect from your work and other similar stressors. The benefits are significant and scientific. Studies show that vigor and performance increase following a rest day, and the more someone actually rests on the weekend, the more effort they expend during the week. If you feel like the ability to take an off-day is out of your control, show this book to your boss and use it to start a sincere discussion about how you need to rest in order to work your best. Nothing makes us more upset than illogical organizations that demand too much and as a result never get enough.

During the process of writing this book, we held each other to taking at least one off-day a week. On that day we didn't write or research a word. Without fail, our strongest writing days occurred on either the next day or 2 days later. (Brad's off-days were generally on Monday. He wrote best on Tuesday and Wednesday.) That we said 2 days later is worth noting. Sometimes it can take both the body and the mind a day to get back into the swing of things. This is why prior to a big Sunday race, many athletes rest on Friday and do a light workout on

A well-timed rest day yields enormous dividends. Rest days allow you to recover from the accumulated stress of the recent past and revitalize you so that you can to push harder in the near future.

Saturday to "wake their body up." This is also why some of the savviest professionals schedule big meetings on Tuesdays instead of Mondays. Some people snap right back from a break, but others take a bit more time. It doesn't take long to figure out which category you fall into, and once you do, a well-timed rest day yields enormous dividends. Rest days allow you to recover from the accumulated stress of the recent past and revitalize you so that you can push harder in the near future.

While rest days are good bridges from week to week, sometimes the body and mind need a longer break. Much like rest days should be strategically timed to follow accumulated stress, so, too, should vacations, albeit on a larger scale. Lagat doesn't take his 5-week hiatus in the middle of the season. He waits until after his last race of the year, when his body and mind are admittedly worn down. For musicians, this may mean taking a break after 50 days on tour or working arduously to complete a record. For visual and material artists, this may mean taking a break after a gallery opening or finishing up an especially challenging piece or series of works. And for intellectuals and business professionals, this may mean timing breaks to follow long periods of work, like the publication of a journal article or book, or the completion of a major investment deal.

We would be remiss not to acknowledge that all kinds of situational factors—from family obligations to financial pressures to workplace policies—can make it hard to intentionally time extended vacations. But to the extent that you can, we encourage you to be thoughtful about when you take your breaks. Research shows that breaks lasting 7 to 10 days have positive effects on motivation, well-being, and health that last up to a month. Other studies

Be thoughtful about when you take your breaks.

have shown that a week-long vacation can diminish or even completely eliminate burnout. But here's the catch: If the conditions that led to burnout in the first place aren't resolved, the symptoms of burnout inevitably return just a few weeks later.

This is an important insight. It means that contrary to common belief, extended breaks are *not* a saving grace that allow people with unsustainable workloads to magically bounce back all chipper. Rather than viewing vacations as a last-ditch tool to save someone on the edge, it's better to think of extended breaks as part of a broader "rest" strategy that includes mini-breaks, sound sleep, and off-days. In other words, when it comes to a comprehensive "rest" strategy, vacations are not the cake—they are merely the icing on top of it, a chance to more fully regroup after accumulating

---

PERFORMANCE PRACTICES

- Regardless of the work you do, take at least 1 off-day every week.
- Time your off-days strategically to follow periods of accumulated stress.
- The more stress, the more rest that is needed.
- To the extent that you can, time your vacations strategically to follow longer periods of stress.
- On both single off-days and extended vacations, truly disconnect from work. Unplug both physically and mentally and engage in activities that you find relaxing and restorative.

---

stress so we can come back stronger and better than before. When Lagat finishes a season, he is fatigued—but he's not broken. Fatigue is a stimulus for growth. Broken is, well, just broken.

THE COURAGE TO REST

The benefits of rest are clear, and they are supported by a large body of scientific evidence. Still, far too few of us get enough of it. It's not that people want to wear themselves down. It's just that we live in a culture that glorifies grinding and nonstop work, even if science says it doesn't make sense. We praise the athlete who stays after practice to pound out additional reps in the weight room, and we lionize the businessperson who sleeps in his office. Now this isn't to suggest that hard work is not paramount to growth. As you saw in Chapter 3, it is. But hopefully by now you also realize that hard work only becomes smart and sustainable work when it's supported by rest. The irony is that resting hard often takes more guts than working hard. Just ask an author like Stephen King ("For me, not working is the real work") or a runner like Deena Kastor ("My workouts are the easy part"). Feelings of guilt and anxiety creep in when we step

Hard work only becomes smart and sustainable work when it's supported by rest.

away from our work, especially if we perceive that our competition is still going at it. Perhaps there is no place where this is truer than at a firm atop the management consulting ladder, Boston Consulting Group (BCG).

BCG regularly ranks as one of the top management consulting firms in the world. The firm's consultants help the CEOs of billion-dollar companies solve their thorniest problems. And the faster BCG consultants can find the answers, the more likely the firm is to get awarded the next multi-million-dollar project. In other words, BCG consultants work in high-stakes, high-pressure environments.

It's not surprising, then, that when researchers proposed a series of experiments to test the effects of required rest on BCG consultants, employees reacted with not just shock but also disdain. The *Harvard Business Review* reported, "The concept was so foreign that [BCG leaders] had to practically force some consultants to take time off, especially when it coincided with periods of peak work intensity." Some consultants legitimately questioned whether being assigned to the experiment was putting their entire careers in jeopardy.

In one experiment, consultants were instructed to take a full day off in the middle of the week. For individuals who usually work 12-plus-hour days, 7 days a week, this was downright absurd. Even the partner who spearheaded the study, herself an emerging believer in the performance-enhancing power of regular rest, became "suddenly nervous about having to tell her client that each member of the team would be off one day a week." She assured the client (and herself) that if the work suffered, she'd immediately call off the experiment.

In a complementary and slightly less radical experiment, a different group of consultants were asked to take 1 night off on a weekday. This meant completely unplugging after 6 p.m. No matter what was happening on the project, there were to be no emails, phone calls, text messages, PowerPoints, or anything else that involved work. This idea, too, was met with staunch resistance. One project manager questioned, "What good is a night off going to do? Won't it just force me to work more on weekends?"

If taking downtime was ever going to fail, it was with this group of high-achieving workaholics who were not shy about expressing their negative bias from the experiment's outset. But as the multi-month experiments unfolded, something unexpected happened. Both groups did a complete flip. By the end of the intervention, all of the consultants who were involved wanted predictable time off. This wasn't just because they experienced benefits in self-care and relationships with family and friends, but also because they were far more productive at work.

Communication between consultants was more efficient and the quality of client deliverables improved. The participants reported that in addition to these near-term benefits, they also felt better about the long-term sustainability of their work. In the words of the researchers overseeing the experiment, "After only five months, consultants on the teams experimenting with time off perceived their work situations more favorably—on every dimension—than their peers on non-experiment teams."

The BCG consultants discovered that it's not just about accumulating hours but about the quality of the work produced in those hours. By working even 20 percent less, the consultants were able to get a lot more done, and feel better about it, too. If BCG consultants—along with the world's best athletes, thinkers, and creatives—can find the courage to rest, so can you. It's not easy, and can feel like quite a leap. But we guarantee that once you start using the strategies noted in this book to interweave rest into your day, week, and year, your performance and vitality will improve.

OVER THE COURSE OF these preceding chapters, we revealed the overarching key to sustainable performance. Those lessons can be simplified using the growth equation: stress + rest = growth. It's a simple yet profound guide to structuring your days, weeks, and years. Just as a coach gives an athlete a bird's-eye view of a training plan, the growth equation provides you a bird's-eye view to improving performance. We cannot emphasize it enough—working in this manner is absolutely key to a lifetime of satisfaction and improvement.

But to more fully understand how to get the most out of ourselves requires that we zoom in and focus on some important details. In the next section, we'll turn to the specific rituals and routines that usher in great performance. We'll explore how prolific writers predictably elicit a state of mind that allows them to crank out thousands of words every day, how the best musicians prepare to perform in front of thousands of screaming fans, and how Olympians ready their minds and bodies to compete on the world's biggest stages. We'll learn that great performers leave nothing to chance. Rather, they engineer particular states of mind and body, and they design their each and every day to get the most out of themselves. And, as you're about to discover, so can you.

> *Stress + rest = growth. It's a simple yet profound guide to structuring your days, weeks, and years.*

PRIMING

6

OPTIMIZE YOUR ROUTINE

att Billingslea is trying to seclude himself in the corner of a crowded locker room. He needs a small space of his own to prepare for what is about to unfold. In just 30 minutes, he'll enter a sold-out stadium to perform in front of thousands of roaring fans. But at the moment, as he completes a calisthenic routine, he looks like a seasoned prizefighter, rhythmically hopping from side to side. This specific routine results from years of practice, tinkering, and repetition. It's become hard-wired, like brushing his teeth in the morning; a must-do before every event.

He begins making wide circles with his arms, gradually increasing speed and intensity. Next, with his back against a wall, he starts raising and lowering his body, activating his core and back muscles. As he cycles through these and other movements, he interweaves active stretching and grip work. His blood is flowing, his joints are loosening, and his muscles are beginning to feel warm. All are signals that his body is ready.

Ten minutes until showtime. Anticipation is growing. His body may be ready, but his mind is still racing. Billingslea shifts his focus to getting into the right headspace. He's taking deep breaths and visualizing his each and every move, how he'll control his body when it's moving at what feels like 100 miles per hour. He is trying to cultivate a specific psychological state, something he calls "the zone." For Billingslea, the zone represents a mindset in which he doesn't dwell on mistakes or get distracted by the crowd. Ideally, he told us, he stops thinking altogether and his performance becomes automatic: "I've done all this work beforehand, but in the moment, I try to get to this sweet spot where I'm not thinking about what I'm doing. I know I've arrived when my mind and body are in perfect sync—it feels effortless, like my performance is just flowing out of me."

Billingslea knows this sweet spot well. He's been in it many times before, and the fluency of his performance tonight and every other night depends upon him accessing it. All of which brings us back to his warmup routine and its sole function: "It gives me the best shot of entering the zone, and of getting there consistently," he explains. In addition to preparing his mind and body, this routine—the same one he's executed for years—helps create a sense of normalcy and predictability, a kind of comfort in a situation that most anyone would find uncomfortable.

Billingslea enters the arena. The lights dim. The roar of the crowd dulls for a brief moment. *Boom!* With a flash of light, the air fills with the sound of over 50,000 eager fans going nuts as international superstar Taylor Swift belts out the lyrics to her latest hit. Billingslea sits just a few feet behind her, hammering away on the drums.

BEFORE BECOMING THE BACKBONE for one of the most popular acts on the planet, Billingslea spent years perfecting his craft. He put in countless hours of deep-focus practice, stressing his mind and body before taking breaks to recover and grow. He played thousands of small gigs in restaurants and bars across the country. He epitomizes gumption, having spent most of his early career forging ahead to a disparaging tune sung not by

Swift but by naysayers who told him, "You won't make it in music." Those years of practice, persistence, and experience—culminating in what we'll call "talent"—serve as the foundation for his performance at each and every stop on Swift's world tour. But in order to fully express his talent, to get the most out of himself on a given particular night, he relies upon a rock-solid routine.

Billingslea isn't alone. Whether it's a writer preparing to draft a story, an athlete prepping for competition, or a businessperson heading into a high-stakes presentation, great performers never just *hope* they'll be on top of their game. Rather, they actively create the specific conditions that will elicit their personal best, priming themselves for performance. As we'll learn in this chapter, these priming strategies are effective because of their specific components and consistent repetition. It's this combination—developing the "right" routine for you and repeating it over and over again—that serves as a gateway to peak performance.

> *Great performers never just hope they'll be on top of their game. Rather, they actively create the specific conditions that will elicit their personal best.*

GET IN THE ZONE

Did you notice anything odd about Billingslea's routine? How about the fact that there was no drumming involved? When we asked Billingslea about this, he told us that he had once moonlighted as a personal trainer. In the same spirit that we, by way of this book, are trying to break down walls between domains, taking knowledge from one and applying it to another, Billingslea began experimenting in his drumming with warmup regimens that he learned from fitness. He found that pushups, jumping jacks, and running in place were as effective at preparing him to play the drums as they were at preparing him to lift weights and run. This makes sense. Drumming consecutively for 2 hours is a physically demanding activity. Billingslea discovered that elevating his heart rate and loosening up his body prior to a show is far more important than warming up the technical aspects of drumming itself. Billingslea already knows how to play the drums. He's got 30 years of experience. Another 30 minutes of practice right before a show isn't going to add much. If anything, it will only detract by making him think more when his goal is to think less. The time during warmup is much better spent ushering in the physical and psychological zone he hopes to enter.

If he were to start the show playing "cold," it would take him the first few songs to enter this state. It doesn't mean he wouldn't get there eventually, but, as he told us, he'd run the risk of "thinking too much early on," which could lead to mistakes and rumination.* In an attempt to minimize that possibility, Billingslea ensures he is already physically alert and psychologically zoned in when he first walks on stage. As a result, he enters the elusive zone more swiftly and predictably. He doesn't wait for the zone to come to him. He creates it. During the climax of a show, when everything is clicking, Billingslea is dripping with sweat as he physically pushes his limits. His mind, by contrast, is in a meditative-like trance.

Another great performer who understands the importance of being ready to go at the start of an event is Megan Gaurnier. Only Gaurnier doesn't hammer on drums; she hammers on pedals. The California-based Olympic cyclist is one of the fastest female riders in the world. She told us that the fitness she's developed through years of training is the bedrock on which her performance lies. But on race day, in order to unlock her fitness, she, too, relies on a routine. "For me, it's yoga. I do the exact same yoga routine every time. It only takes about 20 to 25 minutes, and it predictably puts my body and mind in race mode. It's 100 percent integral to my success when the gun goes off."

Gaurnier isn't alone in her emphasis on routine, particularly when it comes to athletes. Nearly all elite athletes have well-practiced warmup routines that are orchestrated down to the minute. For example, Steve's world-

---

* When Billingslea makes a "mistake," no one else notices, not even other members of the band. Still, he told us that a mistake can really throw him off, which is ironic since no one but he would notice he is "off." It is this relentless pursuit and expectation of personal excellence that epitomizes so many great performers.

class runners know the precise moment during which to begin their pre-race warmup—usually about 60 minutes before competition. They each go through their own carefully crafted sequence, ranging from jogging to dynamic flexibility drills to short sprints. Their goal is the same as Billingslea's and Gaurnier's: to step on the starting line with their bodies and minds in an optimal state. For athletes, a physical warmup does more than stimulate bloodflow and prime the muscles for performance. It also helps to foster a clear and relaxed mind. United States Olympic hero Frank Shorter, the last American to win a gold medal in the marathon (1972), always ate the same exact breakfast—toast, coffee, and fruit—before *every* race, no matter how big or small. In his memoir, *My Marathon: Reflections on a Gold Medal Life,* Shorter wrote, "Consistency was another way to tamp down terror."

You may have noticed variation in the routines we've highlighted thus far. That's because there is no one universal best routine. It's up to you to determine the ideal state of body and mind for the demands of your event, and to figure out the best way to put yourself in, or very close to, that state from the outset. For some this might mean yoga; for others, pushups.

> *It's up to you to determine the ideal state of body and mind for the demands of your event, and to figure out the best way to put yourself in, or very close to, that state from the outset.*

WHILE THIS MAY SEEM IMPORTANT for those who rely on their bodies to perform, what about everyone else? Screenwriter and filmmaker Alexi Pappas, who also happens to be a world-class runner, says she takes the same approach to her creative endeavors as she does to her running:

> *I think the same way I deal with writer's block is the same way I deal with going to [running] practice and warming up for a race. I have these tools and these warmups that I can use to always be able to "show up." Even if you're competing against*

the best runner in the country, you can still do the same warmup for that race and show up in the same way. With writing, I have certain things, like my favorite place to sit or my favorite tea to have. I treat the whole filmmaking thing like it is practice. It's something that I'm committed to. On good days and bad days, you always show up.

Pappas is on to something. Similar to how great athletes prepare their bodies for peak performance, great thinkers and artists prepare their minds.

WARM UP YOUR MIND

Chade-Meng Tan (aka a Jolly Good Fellow, the mindfulness pioneer who you met in Chapter 4) is known for his unique way of entering conference rooms. When Tan first walks into a meeting, he quickly glances around and makes a silent comment to himself about each individual in the room. Unlike the stereotypical corporate operative, Tan isn't sizing everyone up in preparation for white-collar battle. Rather, he's taking a brief moment to say something nice about each person, even if he hasn't yet met them. *Melissa is wonderful to work with . . . Jim is a great marketing manager . . . That lady with red hair looks like she is filled with positive energy . . .* In doing so, Tan is overriding a common instinctive reaction of seeing each person as a potential threat or obstacle. By uttering just a few simple words in his head, Tan primes himself into a positive, cooperative mood.

It turns out that a positive mood is also beneficial for problem solving and creativity. In an experiment out of Northwestern University, participants were given a questionnaire to assess their emotional states. Participants were then divided into two groups based on their mood: one positive and one negative. The subjects in the positive group were significantly more likely to solve challenging intellectual problems with creative insight. In order to find out why, researchers used fMRI scans to watch how the subjects' brains worked as they tried to solve the problems. Those in positive moods demonstrated increased activity in a region of the brain that is associated with decision making and emotional control. This region of the brain is also integral to problem solving (the anterior cingulate cortex). Those in negative moods, however, showed little to no activity in this brain region. In other words, the subjects' ability to activate this critical brain region was linked to their moods. Whereas positive moods were conducive to problem solving and creativity, negative moods inhibited these functions at a deep neurological level. This experiment is just one of many that demonstrates how it is hard to do your best thinking when your mind isn't at peace.

> *It is hard to do your best thinking when your mind isn't at peace.*

The implications are straightforward: You can improve performance by priming yourself into a positive mood prior to important work that involves problem solving and creative thinking. As crazy as it sounds, research shows that something as simple as watching funny cat videos on YouTube can enhance subsequent performance on cognitively-demanding tasks.

Equally as important as conjuring a positive mood is avoiding a negative one. In the interest of upping your performance, try to avoid people, places, and things that may put you in a negative mood. While there are instances when these factors may be out of your control, it is important to realize the impact mood plays on performance. How and with whom you spend your time, especially preceding meaningful work, really matters.

It's also important to remember effect of mood on performance when evaluating yourself and your teammates or colleagues. The latest science suggests it's extremely hard to perform well at work if other elements of your life are not in harmony.

> *Disconnecting "work" from "life" is an illusion.*

Be kind to yourself and others who are going through challenging times, and recognize that disconnecting "work" from "life" is an illusion.

It's not just intellectual or creative work that is influenced by mood; athletic performance is affected by it, too. Consider Tiger Woods, whose golf career took a nosedive at the same time as his personal life did. While Woods's story may be an extreme example, research conducted by exercise scientist Samuele Marcora, PhD, found that even slight and subtle mood influencers can alter athletic performance. In a study involving well-trained cyclists, Marcora flashed either happy or sad faces on a screen as the riders pedaled at an all-out effort. The faces were flashed for just a fraction of a second—so briefly that they could only be recognized by the subconscious. Still, those who were exposed to the happy faces performed 12 percent better than those who were exposed to the sad faces. Marcora's research serves as further proof that mood has profound effects on performance deep inside our brains and bodies. His experimental findings also support years of anecdotal evidence that athletes tend to perform best when everything is clicking not just on the field but also off it.

Though we've focused predominantly on mood, there are numerous other opportunities for psychological priming. For example, during the process of writing this book, whenever we hit an impasse that we couldn't overcome with a standard break or, even worse, felt writer's block looming, we turned to reading our favorite books in genres similar to this one.* Without fail, rereading these books helped to jumpstart our creative-writing minds. We weren't surprised when we later learned that in an actual study (similar to our self-experiment), researchers found that subjects improved pattern recognition ability, a common indicator of general cognitive performance, by 37 percent after reading well-written prose.

The lesson is not necessarily to surround your working space with smiley faces or to watch comedy prior to your next big event (though these practices certainly wouldn't hurt). The lesson is, however, that your mental state preceding a performance can considerably affect it. Much like Billingslea, Gaurnier, and other world-class athletes who design preperformance routines to prepare their bodies and focus their minds, you, too, can design a preperformance routine to help you deliver your best.

---

* In particular, *The Upside of Stress* by Kelly McGonigal, PhD, *Give and Take* by Adam Grant, *The Sports Gene* by David Epstein, *Quiet* by Susan Cain, *Drive* by Daniel Pink, and *Presence* by Amy Cuddy.

PERFORMANCE PRACTICES

- Reflect upon the activities in your life that are most important to you.

- Determine what state of mind and/or body they demand.

- Prime yourself for performance by readying your mind and/or body prior to key activities.

- Test and refine various priming techniques, eventually developing customized routines.

- Be consistent: Use the same routine each and every time you engage in the activity to which it is linked (more on the importance of consistency in a bit).

- Remember the impact of mood on performance; positivity goes a long way.

ENVIRONMENT MATTERS

In the process of writing this book, we relied not only on reading our favorite books but also on coffee. Lots of coffee. And not just any coffee, but the same drink, at the same coffee shop, at the same table, at the same time of day, each and every day. Additionally, we each had music playlists devoted solely to writing, and Brad went as far as having a separate computer that he used only for working on this book. Though on first blush it may seem like we were falling prey to our type-A tendencies, this wasn't the case. Rather, we were following the advice of one of the most prolific writers ever, Stephen King.

Everything about King's writing setup is intentional, from the room he writes in to the placement of his desk to the materials on it to the blasting AC/DC, Metallica, and Guns N' Roses that he writes to. There is no particular secret to King's setup, and it's certainly not the best one for everyone (we couldn't imagine writing to heavy metal, for instance). What is important, however, is that he has created an environment that works for him. In his memoir, *On Writing,* King puts it simply: "Most of us do our best work in a place of our own."

King's sentiment is not unique. Nearly every great performer you'll meet in this book emphasized the importance of *where* they perfect their craft.

> *The specific places in which we work matter.*

From a world-class athlete's favorite gym, to an award-winning artist's customized studio, to King's writing cave, the specific places in which we work matter. An obscure field called ecological psychology sheds insight into why this is the case.

Ecological psychology suggests that the objects that surround us are not static; rather, they influence and invite specific behaviors. Experiments show that the mere sight of an object elicits brain activity associated with particular actions. For example, when we see an image of a chair, the parts of our brain responsible for coordinating the act of sitting (i.e., motor programs) start firing, even if we haven't physically moved at all. It's as if the chair is speaking to us, saying, "Hey, come have a seat," and our brains are listening and responding accordingly. This phenomenon helps explain why athletes in action sports, like football, often report that they don't "think" about which direction to run; the linear process of reasoning would take far too long. Rather, when a gap opens up on the football field it literally invites players, on a level far deeper than what they experience in their consciousness, to run through it.

Put simply, we are not as separate from our surroundings as we may think. Instead, our brains are engaged in an intricate conversation with the objects that surround us, and the more they converse, the tighter the back and forth becomes. The first time a baby sees a chair, for example, the motor programs in her brain do not automatically begin to fire in a sitting pattern. But by the time that baby is an adult and she has seen and sat in thousands of chairs, the sight of a chair invites a sitting response deep inside her brain.

This concept may seem a bit esoteric, but the practical implications are down to earth and simple. When we create a space in which to practice

---

PERFORMANCE PRACTICES

- Create "a place of your own" in which you do your most important work.
- Surround yourself with objects that invite your desired behaviors.
- Consistently work in that same place, using the same materials.
- Over time, your environment will enhance your productivity on a deep neurological level.

---

our craft, it is beneficial to surround ourselves with objects that invite desired actions and eliminate ones that do not. In his book *The Evolving Self*, Mihaly Csikszentmihalyi, PhD, writes that being intentional about our surroundings is essential to eliciting our best performance. The things we work among, he writes, become "expansions of the self . . . things the mind can use to create harmony in experience."

Furthermore, by working in the same environment consistently and repeatedly, the bond between us and our surroundings tightens. The work of behavioral neuroscientist Daniel Levitin, PhD, supports Brad's use of a writing-only computer. According to Levitin, when an object, like a computer, is isolated for a specific task, like writing, the link between subject (writer) and object (computer) strengthens. Over time, the mere sight of that specific computer invites writing, literally nudging Brad's brain to think about the book/story/article he is working on.

> *The things we work amidst become expansions of the self, things the mind can use to create harmony in experience.*

STRATEGIC ROUTINES go far beyond superstitions, like wearing the same socks or underwear before a big event. Rather, the activities we do prior to performing prime our bodies and our minds into specific states, and the environments we work in invite and influence certain behaviors. When we repeatedly execute the same routine and work in the same environment, we create strong links deep inside our brains and bodies. We connect what we do before we work and where we work to the act of working itself. Essentially, we condition ourselves to work.

CONDITIONING

You already read that Stephen King is meticulous about his writing routine and environment. As a result, whenever King sits down to write, he is primed for productivity. King doesn't believe in happenstance or that inspiration mysteriously strikes. "Don't wait for the muse," King writes in his memoir. "Your job is to make sure the muse knows where you are going to be every day from nine 'til noon or seven 'till three. If he knows," King writes, "I assure you he'll start showing up."

> *"Your schedule exists in order to habituate yourself, to make yourself ready to dream just as you make yourself ready to sleep by going to bed at roughly the same time each night and following the same ritual as you go."*

Much like the drummer Matt Billingslea uses his routine to predictably bring about the "zone" or the cyclist Megan Gaurnier uses her routine to ready her mind and body for bike racing, King relies upon his routine for a consistent stream of creativity. "Your schedule—in at about the same time every day, out when your thousand words are on paper or disk—exists in order to habituate yourself, to make yourself ready to dream just as you make yourself ready to sleep by going to bed at roughly the same time each night and following the same ritual as you go."

King's reliance on ritual is nothing new among great thinkers. Another notable example is the psychologist B.F. Skinner, PhD. In the early 1960s, when Skinner was completing his most groundbreaking intellectual work, he adhered to an exacting routine. In a 1963 journal entry, he wrote:

I rise sometimes between 6 and 6:30 often having heard the radio news. My breakfast, a dish of corn flakes, is on the kitchen table. Coffee is made automatically by the stove timer. I breakfast alone . . . at seven or so I go down to my study, a walnut-paneled room in our basement. My work desk is a long Scandinavian-modern table, with a set of shelves I made myself for holding the works of BFS, dictionaries, word-books, etc. . . . . Later in the morning I go to my office. These days I leave just before 10 so that Debbie can ride with me to her summer school class . . .

And on he went, outlining, nearly down to the minute, the precise details of his each and every day.

Skinner was the ultimate creature of habit. He even began and ended his writing sessions with the buzz of a timer. The great irony, of course, is that Skinner was using the power of routine to help him develop the psychological theory underpinning the power of routine: behaviorism. At its core, behaviorism suggests that certain actions can be triggered, or "conditioned," by external cues. Skinner's most well-known feats of conditioning involved teaching rats to pull levers and pigeons to play ping-pong. He taught the small animals by associating the desired behaviors with food. (Anyone who has ever trained a pet using food has Skinner to thank.)

Skinner believed that nearly any trigger could elicit certain behaviors so long as the two (i.e., trigger and behavior) were consistently paired and positively reinforced. Under the lens of behaviorism, Skinner's own painstaking routine served as a trigger to cue the behavior of writing, which was reinforced by the positive emotions he felt after being productive.

Modern psychology accepts that human behavior is far more complex than Skinner's behaviorism. But the theory's essence lives on through the in-vogue science of habits, which is that behaviors can be cued by the activities that precede them. Perhaps today we wouldn't say that Billingslea, Gaurnier, and King use their routines to "condition" performance. Instead, we'd say they "make a habit" out of excellence. But it's really two sides of the same coin.

PERFORMANCE PRACTICES

- Link key behaviors to specific cues and/or routines.

- Be consistent and frequent; execute the same cue/routine every time prior to the behavior to which it is paired.

- If possible, link key activities to the same context (e.g., time of day, physical environment, etc.).

- If your pursuit requires variable settings, develop portable cues/routines that can be executed anywhere (e.g., a deep-breathing routine, self-talk, etc.).

- Consistency is king. The best routine means nothing if you don't regularly practice it.

By consistently linking our work to the same routine (and, when possible, to the same environment) great performance starts to become more automatic.

FROM PSYCHOLOGY TO BIOLOGY

Dave Hamilton's British accent stands out on the practice field in Lancaster, Pennsylvania, where he is the director of performance science for the US women's field hockey team. Hamilton is charged with ending the US team's medal drought, which dates back to 1984. Only recently was Hamilton recruited from the United Kingdom, where he helped lead the UK women's field hockey team to a bronze medal in the 2012 Olympics.

Much like the US squad, prior to 2012, the Brits, too, were in a drought, having not won a medal in 20 years. Despite all indicators signaling world-class performance, the British team struggled in critical matches; they were champions of training, but they couldn't put it together on game day. An exercise scientist himself, Hamilton took a meticulous approach to figuring out why his women couldn't translate their exemplary training into exemplary performance.

Hamilton tracked everything, starting with his athletes' training regimes. No red flags emerged. This wasn't surprising given the high level of play he observed at each and every practice. Altering his athletes' physiology wasn't the answer. But, Hamilton wondered, what about altering their biology? Could that give his women the extra edge they needed on game day?

In particular, Hamilton was curious about the hormone testosterone. Perhaps more than any other hormone, testosterone is linked to performance. It increases muscle growth, strength, and energy. In addition to its profound effects on our physiology, testosterone is also linked to enhanced creativity, confidence, memory, and attention. In other words, testosterone is a potent performance enhancer across nearly all endeavors. And while synthetic testosterone is banned from sports, Hamilton believed he could increase the natural amount of testosterone already coursing through his athletes' bodies.

Hamilton began by doubling down on sleep, ensuring that his athletes were all getting at least 8 hours a night (for more on sleep and testosterone, see Chapter 5). But he went far beyond sleep, measuring, via salivary tests, how just about everything impacted his athletes' testosterone levels. For example, he evaluated how testosterone responded to negative versus positive feedback, pregame speeches, inspirational films, social surroundings, and sprint versus endurance warmups.

Hamilton found there was no single formula for increasing testosterone levels. Rather, the athletes' responses to different stimuli varied: For example, some experienced spikes in testosterone after running short and fast, whereas others got a boost after running long and slow; some had higher testosterone levels after prepping for games on their own, whereas others benefited from warming up in a group, and so forth. What remained constant, however, was that elevating pregame testosterone significantly improved the athletes' performance. They key to Hamilton's conundrum, and ultimately to an Olympic medal for the UK women's field hockey team, was increasing the testosterone levels in his athletes.

With that in mind, prior to the 2012 Olympics Hamilton worked with each of his athletes to develop individualized pregame routines. He ensured each athlete's routine was "optimal" by measuring their testosterone when he tweaked their routine. By the time the 2012 Games rolled around, every athlete had a custom routine designed specifically to maximize her testosterone. The unconventional approach worked, as evidenced by the team's Olympic medal that year.

While Hamilton used repeated tests to develop his athletes' routines, such an extreme level of precision might not have been necessary. Without fail, he told us, testosterone levels were highest when his athletes felt good. So, he said, "When it came to performance on game day, everything we did was to make each and every individual athlete feel confident that her mind and body were ready when the whistle blew."

EARLIER IN THIS CHAPTER, we learned that routines are so effective because they prompt specific behaviors and physical and psychological states. What Hamilton's story adds is that an individualized routine goes beyond just priming us to work. It also alters our biology, changing our hormonal profile in a manner that increases strength, energy, confidence, creativity, attention, and memory. In other words, developing a custom routine doesn't just condition us to perform. It enhances the performance itself.

If stress + rest = growth is the foundation upon which our talent is built, then our routines and environments help us to fully express that talent.

7

MINIMALIST TO
BE A MAXIMALIST

Michael Joyner, MD, a physician and researcher at the prestigious Mayo Clinic, is not only an expert on human performance, he's also a great performer himself. Joyner has published more than 350 articles on the topic and has won numerous awards for his work. Recently, he was named the distinguished investigator at the Mayo Clinic and was awarded a grant through the celebrated Fulbright Scholar Program. In addition to his research, Joyner, an anesthesiologist, sees patients regularly and is a mentor to countless up-and-comers, informally running what he calls "my own version of a Montessori school." He writes for *Sports Illustrated* magazine and is frequently cited as an expert in other leading publications. If that isn't enough, Joyner (now 58) is still an avid athlete himself, and in his heyday he ran marathons at blazing speeds. To top it all off, he's married with young kids.

Joyner doesn't have a special genetic mutation that gives him endless energy, nor does he work 12-hour days. He does, however, minimize distractions and eliminate activities that are extraneous to his work. This isn't to say Joyner is narrow-minded, walled off in his own field. If anything, he is quite the opposite. "I block off between 60 and 90 minutes every day to read outside of my domain," he told us. "This helps me generate new ideas." But Joyner only does this extensive reading because he identified creativity as something integral to his research, and reading broadly is one of his conduits to creativity. He doesn't expend time or energy on anything that is not critical to his mission. "In order to be a maximalist," he says, "you have to be a minimalist." Take note: This does not mean you should aspire to be narrow or overly specialized. As we've seen in this book, many great performers have diverse interests that work together to feed their success. What this does mean, however, is that you should identify and strive to cut out all the superficial things in your life. You should be fully intentional with how you spend your most precious resource of all: time.

In order to be a maximalist, you have to be a minimalist.

A day in the life of Joyner exemplifies this philosophy. He rises early, between 4:30 and 5:00 a.m., well before his wife or young kids are awake. During this sacred hour, when his mind is freshest and he is wholly undistracted, he completes what he feels is his most pressing and important work for that day. By the time his family awakes, he is ready for a break, so he shifts to spending quality time with them. An hour later, when he heads out for the day, he grabs a prepacked gym bag filled with the same set of workout clothes and the same set of work clothes as it is every day. "I don't want to devote any brainpower to thinking about what to wear," he told us. He proceeds to ride his bike to a gym located near his office, which is only a few miles away. "I was very intentional about selecting where to live," he said. "I didn't want to waste time commuting, nor burn willpower dealing with traffic. So I chose a place that is a short bike ride away. Plus, on days when I can't get to the gym, my bike commute ensures I complete at least some physical activity."

At work, Joyner doesn't engage in politics or office gossip. And while there are countless seminars and conferences that he could attend literally every day, he often chooses not to, as they would detract from his deep-focus work. When Joyner returns home in the evening, he does his best to "turn it off," rarely, if ever, engaging in extracurricular activities. In order to do great work, he told us, "You need to say no to a lot of things so that when it's time to say yes, you can do so with all your energy." Joyner will be the first to tell you that saying no isn't easy. "I could have lived in New York, Boston, or Washington DC," he explained, "but I was attracted to Rochester, Minnesota, because it was a place where I could most easily focus on what is most important to me: my research and family." And since Joyner loves both his research and family, he's extremely happy.

Joyner has designed not only his days but, really, his entire life around eliminating distractions and decisions "that don't really matter." In doing so, he reserves energy and willpower for the activities that are critically important to him. In other words, the secret to Joyner's accomplishing so much, to being a "maximalist" in his field, is that he is a "minimalist" in nearly everything else.

If Joyner's philosophy and lifestyle sound familiar, that's because they are similar to that of another great performer we met in Chapter 3: Bob Kocher, MD. Dr. Bob compartmentalizes his day down to the minute, ensuring that each compartment has a distinct purpose. Like Joyner, Dr. Bob is very intentional about what he does and doesn't do, where he does and doesn't devote his energy. Emil Alzamora, an award-winning artist who you'll learn more about later on, built his studio, what he calls his "cave," in his backyard. He did this, he told us, "to minimize what stands between me and my art." It is this sort of intentionality that Alzamora, Dr. Bob, Joyner, and so many other great performers share. Great performers choose where to focus their energy, and they protect it from everything else that could encroach upon it. This includes even seemingly simple things, like deciding what style of shirt to wear.

DECISION FATIGUE

Next time you are at your computer, take a moment and complete a Google-image search of Facebook founder and CEO Mark Zuckerberg. (By now you know we'd rather you not reach for your smartphone, but proceed if you must.) Odds are, you'll notice something similar about the pictures. Outside of very rare occasions when he is required to do otherwise, Zuckerberg almost always dons the same outfit: blue jeans, a gray T-shirt, and a hooded sweatshirt. It's not that Zuckerberg is trying to make a fashion statement, promoting a relaxed dress code to Silicon Valley (though he's certainly done that). Rather, his limited wardrobe is founded in an effort to increase his productivity and enhance his performance.

At the end of 2014, in Zuckerberg's first-ever public Q&A session, the question that garnered the most attention was, "Why do you wear the same T-shirt every day?"

"I really want to clear my life to make it so that I have to make as few decisions as possible about anything except how to best serve this community," replied Zuckerberg, clarifying that he had "multiple same shirts." He went on to explain that, when taken together, small decisions—like choosing what to wear—add up and can be quite tiring. "I'm in this really lucky position, where I get to wake up every day and help serve more than a billion people. And I feel like I'm not doing my job if I spend any of my energy on things that are silly or frivolous about my life," he said.

Zuckerberg isn't the first genius to simplify his wardrobe. Many say that Albert Einstein, like Zuckerberg, had a closet filled with "multiple same gray suits." Steve Jobs almost exclusively wore a black mock turtleneck, blue jeans, and New Balance sneakers. President Barack Obama recently told *Vanity Fair* magazine, "You'll see I wear only the same gray or blue suits. I'm trying to pare down decisions. I don't want to make decisions about what I'm eating or wearing because I have too many other decisions to make." We could go on and on about the countless other great performers who have eliminated trivial decisions from their lives. But can removing such simple choices—blue shirt or red shirt, Apple Jacks or Cheerios—truly affect performance?

Recall the notion of our mind as a muscle, the theory pioneered by psychologist Roy Baumeister, PhD, that we introduced in Chapter 1 suggesting that we have a limited reservoir of mental energy, which, over the course of a day, becomes depleted as we use it.* Initially, research on this theory focused mainly on self-control: how resisting temptations early in the day makes us more likely to give in to them later on. But scientists soon found that it isn't only resisting temptations that wears us out, but also making decisions.

Judges are charged with making impartial decisions based only on the evidence at hand. We expect judges to be skilled at minimizing noise and bias, evaluating each case in a vacuum. That's why it is especially surprising that research shows judges' rulings are heavily influenced by the number of decisions they previously made. For example, one study found that judges granted prisoners parole 65 percent of the time at the beginning of the day, but nearly zero percent of the time at the end of the day. These judges were succumbing to something called "decision fatigue." As the decisions they were forced to make accumulated, the judges became mentally tired and thus had less energy to think critically about cases, opting instead for the easier default choice of no parole.

Judges are not the only professionals who are respected for their ability to think critically but suffer from decision fatigue. A recent study found that physicians make significantly more prescribing errors as the day wears on. Jeffrey Linder, MD, lead author on the study, told the *New York Times*, "The radical notion here is that doctors are people too, and we may be fatigued and make worse decisions toward the end of our clinic sessions."

Without doubt, evaluating whether to grant parole or examining a sick patient requires a lot more thought than deciding what color shirt to wear. Nonetheless, even seemingly trivial decisions deplete us. Experiments show that people who were forced to make choices among a range of consumer goods (e.g., color of T-shirt, type of scented candle, brand of

---

* One of the best ways to "restore" willpower is to take a break from the demanding task. This explains why we generally wake up with a full tank of willpower in the morning—for most of us, sleep is our longest break.

shampoo, type of candy, and, yes, even type of sock) performed worse than those who were presented with only one option on tests of everything from physical stamina to persistence to problem-solving. The subjects who were confronted with multiple choices also procrastinated more in other areas of their life later on in the day. The researchers involved in these studies concluded that even when it comes to the simplest things, "making many decisions leaves a person in a depleted state," impairing his performance on future activities.

Each time we make a deliberate decision, however inconsequential it may seem, our brain is processing different scenarios and evaluating all the options. As the decisions we make add up, so, too, does the amount of processing required by our brain. Just like any other muscle would, our mental muscle gets tired.* In addition to fatiguing us over the course of a day, making decisions, even small ones, interrupts our

> *We should realize we have limited energy and devote it only to things that really matter.*

acute train of thought. Our brains must drop whatever they were currently stewing on (or, if our brains were in a creative mind-wandering state, they must switch out of it into an effortful thinking state) all just to evaluate what kind of socks we should wear.

This doesn't mean that we should live on autopilot, opting to make hardly any decisions at all. But it does mean we should realize that we have limited energy and devote it only to things that really matter. Of course, the more things that we think really matter, the less energy we have to devote to any one of them. It is only by becoming a minimalist that we can become a maximalist.

The key to being a minimalist is making a routine out of just about

---

* Our mental muscle is responsible not only for our ability to think critically but also for our self-control. This means that even if your endeavor is physical in nature (e.g., running or weightlifting), your ability to push yourself to the max—one of the most challenging expressions of self-control there is—may depend on the decisions you made (or didn't make) earlier in the day. In other words, regardless of what it is that you do, eliminating nonessential decision making can enhance your performance. This is why many coaches do what they can to ensure athletes have nothing to think about on game day.

everything that is not core to your mission. When decisions are automatic, you skip the conscious deliberation and associated brain activity. You move straight from encountering a situation (e.g., I need to get dressed) to performing an action (e.g., putting on the same shirt as I do every day) without expending energy in between. In a sense, you are cheating fatigue, saving your mental muscle for things that actually matter to you. The more decisions you make automatic, the more energy you'll have for the work you deem important. The most essential part about adopting the

PERFORMANCE PRACTICES

- Become a minimalist to be a maximalist.
- Reflect on all the decisions that you make throughout a day.
- Identify ones that are unimportant, that don't really matter to you.
- Automate as many of the decisions that don't really matter as you can. Common examples include decisions about:

  ✓ Clothing

  ✓ What to eat at meals

  ✓ When to complete daily activities (e.g., always exercise at the same time of the day so you literally don't need to think about it)

  ✓ Whether to attend social gatherings (It's not *always* a good idea, but during important periods of work, many great performers adopt a strict policy of saying no to social events.)

- In addition to eliminating as many decisions as possible, don't devote brainpower to gossip, politics, or worrying about what others think of you. (Unless, of course, your core mission is to be an elected official—then these things are, in fact, critically important.)
- In addition to reflecting upon daily decisions, think about the second- and third-order effects (e.g., commute time, financial pressures, etc.) of larger life decisions, like where to live.

minimalist-to-be-a-maximalist lifestyle, then, is figuring out what really matters to you—what is actually worth expending energy on—and devoting minimal energy to everything else.

LARKS AND OWLS

If the first step to designing an optimal day is figuring out *what* to do (and, perhaps more important, what not to do), then the second step is figuring out *when* to do it. In his book *Daily Rituals*, author Mason Currey detailed a typical day for more than 50 of the world's greatest artists, writers, musicians, and thinkers to ever live. Not surprisingly, nearly all of them were minimalists, and they all adhered to fairly rigid routines. But the routines themselves, how these great performers designed their days, varied significantly. This was especially true for *when* they did their best work. Some, including Mozart, did their best work late into the night. Others, including Beethoven, were most productive at the crack of dawn. The take-home message wasn't that the majority of these great performers did their best work at a certain time of day, or that there is an optimal hour for productivity. Rather, each individual figured out when they were most alert and focused, and designed their day accordingly. These individuals were optimizing around their respective chronotypes, which is the scientific term for the unique ebb and flow of energy that everyone experiences over the course of 24 hours.

Scientists refer to those who are most alert in the morning as "larks" and those who are most alert in the evening as "owls." Numerous studies confirm that these categories are indeed very real. Whether they be physically or cognitively demanding tasks, most people tend to perform their best either in the earlier part of the day (i.e., larks) or in the later part of the day (i.e., owls). These individual differences are rooted in our bodies' unique biological rhythms—when various hormones associated with energy and focus are released, and when our body temperatures rise and fall. While some of us get pulses of energizing hormones earlier in the day, they come later on for others.

DETERMINING YOUR CHRONOTYPE

To help determine your chronotype, you can use an evidence-based questionnaire designed by researchers from the Sleep Research Center at Loughborough University in the UK. While information on how to access the full version is in the Bibliography and Source Notes and portion of this book, answering the three questions here should give you a good idea of where you fall on the lark-owl spectrum.

1. If you were entirely free to set up your evening, with no commitments in the morning, what time would you go to sleep?

2. You have to do 2 hours of physically hard work. If you were entirely free to plan your day, when would you do this work?

3. You have to take a 2-hour test, which you know will be mentally exhausting. If you were entirely free to choose, when would you choose to take the test?

This questionnaire is a valuable tool, but the best way to understand your optimal schedule is to listen to your body. For the next 2 days, pay deep attention to when your energy levels feel the highest and when you fall into that foggy brain state in which attention lags and your work starts to suffer.

While a 2-day reflective period can be insightful, months of coffee, sugar, and "fighting" fatigue can mess with your chronotype. Thus, the gold-standard way to learn your chronotype is to go 7 days without setting an alarm clock or compensating for fatigue at any point of the day. Not only will you most accurately home in on your chronotype, but you'll also benefit from a "reset" period during which your body can return to its natural rhythm.

You could undergo extensive longitudinal bloodwork to figure out when you're most likely to be at your best, or you could save the money and hassle and just ask yourself some key questions. All of the great performers with whom we spoke while writing this book told us that there were specific times when they did their best work and, outside of a few Olympians, they didn't rely on blood tests to figure out when those times were. They simply engaged in a bit of introspection.

While we perform best on work that demands deep focus and attention during our peak hours (i.e., mornings for larks and evenings for owls), the opposite holds true for generating creative ideas. As we learned in Chapter 4, creativity often requires stepping away from whatever it is we are working on and letting our minds wander. In doing so, we unleash the creative power of our subconscious (our brain's default-mode network). During our peak hours, when we are hyper-alert and focused, our conscious mind is dominant. But during our off-peak hours, as we become fatigued and struggle to maintain focus, our more creative mind has a better opportunity to shine. It should come as no surprise, then, that researchers have found larks perform best on tasks requiring creative insight in the evening, whereas owls tend to be most creative in the morning.

Over time, we (Steve and Brad) discovered that we are larks and designed our writing days accordingly. We used mornings to edit and refine writing (deep-focus work) and afternoons to work on new ideas and the next phase of writing (creative work). This allowed for a nice cycle: refining in the morning the raw and creative work we completed the prior afternoon.

Great performers don't fight their body's natural rhythm; rather, they take advantage of it. They intentionally schedule their hardest and most demanding deep-focus work (or, for athletes, their workouts) during periods in which they are the most alert. For some this is early in the morning and for others this is late at night. When their biology shifts and they become less alert, great performers focus on tasks that, while still integral to their work, demand less attention. These tasks include things like responding to emails, scheduling unavoidable yet highly unproductive meetings, or doing basic chores around the house. Finally, when their attention really begins to wane, they don't "force" themselves to keep work-

---

PERFORMANCE PRACTICES

- Determine your chronotype using the previous tools and suggestions.
- Design your day accordingly—be very intentional about when you schedule certain activities, matching the demands of the activity with your energy level.
  - ✓ Protect the time during which you are most alert and use it for your most important work.
  - ✓ Schedule less demanding tasks during periods in which you are less alert.
  - ✓ Don't fight fatigue! Rather, use this time for recovery and to generate creative ideas that you can act on during your next cycle of high energy and focus.
- Work in alignment with your chronotype—it not only maximizes performance, but it also helps to ensure an appropriate balance between stress and rest.

---

ing. Rather, great performers let their minds wander and their bodies recover, and in doing so, they often experience "aha" or "eureka" moments of insight. In other words, great performers are highly aware of their unique chronotypes and do everything they can to align their activities with their energy levels. You can strive to do the same.

CHOOSE YOUR FRIENDS WISELY

In 2010, the United States Air Force Academy set out to understand why some cadets increase their fitness during their time at the Academy while others do not. In a National Bureau of Economic Research study that tracked a cohort of cadets over 4 years, researchers found that while there was variability in fitness gains/losses across all the cadets, there was hardly any variability within squadrons. Squadrons are groups of about 30 cadets to which an individual is randomly assigned prior to his freshman year. Cadets spend the vast majority of their time interacting with peers in their squadron. In a sense, the squadron becomes a second family: Cadets in the same squadron eat, sleep, study, and work out together. Even though all the squadrons trained and recovered in exactly the same manner, some squadrons showed vast increases in fitness over 4 years whereas others did not.

It turns out the determining factor as to whether the 30 cadets within a squadron improved was the motivation of the least fit person in the group. If the least fit person was motivated to improve, then his enthusiasm spread and everyone improved. If, on the other hand, the least fit person was apathetic or, worse, negative, he dragged everyone down. Just like diseases easily spread through tight-knit groups, so does motivation. And it's quite contagious.

Just like diseases easily spread through tight-knit groups, so does motivation.

Even the simple act of observing others can affect your own motivation. Researchers at the University of Rochester had subjects watch a video of someone describing themselves as being either intrinsically motivated (i.e., motivation comes from within) or extrinsically motivated (i.e., motivation comes from external recognition and rewards) to play a game. Those who were assigned to watch the video of people describing themselves as being intrinsically motivated reported feeling more intrinsically motivated themselves. Furthermore, when researchers left the subjects alone, those who had watched the intrinsic video started playing (of their own volition) the same game shown in the video, while those who watched the extrinsic video did not. Perhaps most fascinating is that these effects were strong irrespective of whether someone identified as being intrinsically or extrinsically motivated prior to the experiment. It's as if your own attitude pales in comparison to the attitudes of those around you.

Motivation isn't the only emotion that is contagious. Research shows that when we see someone else express happiness or sadness (e.g., by smiling or frowning), the neural networks associated with those emotions become active in our own brains. The same goes for pain; the mere sight of someone in pain activates our own neurological pain response. This explains why we

> *The makeup of your social circle has profound implications for your own behavior.*

cry during sad movies, feel uplifted among happy friends, and cringe when we bear witness to someone in pain. In the words of Stanford University psychologist Emma Seppälä, PhD, "We are wired for empathy."

Not only are we wired for empathy, but there is strong evidence that we have socially contagious emotions that prompt very concrete actions and behaviors. Studies show that if one of your friends becomes obese, you are 57 percent more likely to become obese yourself. If one of your friends quits smoking cigarettes, the chances you'll smoke decrease by 36 percent. These social influences remain surprisingly strong even in the case of second- and third-degree connections. If a friend of a friend becomes obese, your odds of gaining weight increase by 20 percent. Even if an acquaintance you barely know starts smoking, it affects the chances you'll light up by 11 percent. In other words, the makeup of your social circle has profound implications for your own behavior. While *what* you do and *when* you do it is important, so is *who* you do it with.

AT THE PEAK OF the Greek Empire, Plato noted, "What is honored in a country will be cultivated there." The same holds true for a team or social group. When sports teams go on winning streaks, there is almost always talk of a magical chemistry that flows through the locker room. Often, it's not the team that has the largest collection of

> *What is honored in a country will be cultivated there. The same holds true for a team or social group.*

pure talent that wins championships, but the team that is best able to come together. It is no different off the athletic field. In the words of business and management guru Peter Drucker, "Culture eats strategy for breakfast."

PERFORMANCE PRACTICES

- Recognize the enormous power of the people with whom you surround yourself.

- Positive energy, motivation, and drive are all contagious. Do what you can to cultivate your own village of support, to surround yourself with a culture of performance.

- Remember that by being positive and showing motivation, you are not only helping yourself, but you are also helping everyone else in your life.

- Unfortunately, negativity and pessimism are also contagious. Don't put up with too much of either. A chain is only as strong as its weakest link.

While we don't all work on teams, the significance of who we surround ourselves with is universally important. Who we interact with day in and day out, who we turn to when the going gets tough, and who we share our working spaces with—all of these things have a profound impact on how we feel and perform. If we are constantly working against the mindset of those who surround us, it's only a matter of time before we, too, will get dragged down, just like some of the Air Force cadets did.* If, on the other hand, we surround ourselves with those who support, motivate, and challenge us, we can reach greater heights than we could have alone. In the words of the Olympic cyclist Megan Gaurnier, "I cannot stress enough the importance of building a 'village' of the right personal and professional supporters—it's everything."

> *If we surround ourselves with those who support, motivate, and challenge us, we can reach greater heights than we could have alone.*

---

* Apathy and negativity are particularly dangerous in the face of challenge. An apathetic or negative peer exploits and amplifies preexisting doubts one might have.

SHOWING UP

The best performers design their days strategically: They are minimalists in order to be maximalists; they ensure their work is in harmony with their chronotype; and they surround themselves with supportive, like-minded people. But designing the perfect day means nothing if you don't show up for it. In the words of the writer James Clear, "The single greatest skill in any endeavor is doing the work. Not doing the work that is easy for you. Not doing the work that makes you look good. Not doing the work when you feel inspired. Just doing the work."

> The best performers are not consistently great, but they are great at being consistent.

The best performers are not consistently great, but they are great at being consistent. They show up every day and they do the work. A large body of social science suggests that attitudes often follow behaviors. Great performers understand this and, if nothing more, they make sure to at least get started on all their working days.

When drafting a novel, award-winning author Haruki Murakami designs his day with precision and adheres to a strict routine. But he'll be the first to tell you that the routine itself is really just there to support what matters most—showing up. He'll also be the first to tell you that showing up isn't easy:

> When I'm in writing mode for a novel, I get up at 4 a.m. and work for 5 to 6 hours. In the afternoon, I run 4 kilometers or swim for 1,500 meters (or do both), then I read a bit and listen to some music. I go to bed at 9 p.m. I keep to this routine every day without variation. The repetition itself becomes the important thing; it's a form of mesmerism. I mesmerize myself to reach a deeper state of mind. But to hold such repetition for so long—6 months to a year—requires a good amount of mental and physical strength. In that sense, writing a novel is like survival training. Physical strength is as necessary as artistic sensitivity.

The real secret of world-class performers isn't the daily routines that they develop, but that they stick to them. That they show up, even when they don't feel like it.

If you think about it, everything we've discussed in this chapter works in service of showing up and being at your best when you do. Perhaps the real secret of world-class performers is not the daily routines that they develop, but that they stick to them. That they show up, even when they don't feel like it. Call it drive, call it passion, or call it grit; whatever you call it, it must come from deep within. But, in an interesting twist, this strength that comes from deep within is often rooted in something "without." When the going gets tough, great performers don't show up for themselves. They show up for something greater than themselves. As a matter of fact, they transcend the very notion of the "self" altogether. That's where we'll turn next.

PURPOSE

8

TRANSCEND YOUR "SELF"

s soon as Tom Boyle heard the panic in his wife's voice, he knew something was gravely wrong. "Oh my gosh! Tom! Tom! Did you see that?" she screamed.

What Tom and his wife had both just witnessed was Kyle Holtrust, an 18-year-old boy, hit head-on by a Chevy Camaro while he was riding his bike on a suburban road in Tucson, Arizona. When Boyle ran to the scene of the crash, he noticed the car's two front wheels were elevated ever so slightly off the ground. Before he could fully register what was happening, he heard screams: "Get me out, get me out! It hurts! Get me out!" Holtrust was alive, but trapped underneath the crushing weight of the car.

Without thinking, Boyle began lifting the front end of the Camaro. Holtrust continued to scream, "Higher! Higher!" Boyle kept lifting. After what seemed like hours, Boyle heard Holtrust gasp, "Okay. It's off me, but I can't move. I can't move my legs. Get me out. Please! Please get me out."

With this, unfortunately Boyle couldn't help. His hands were full—with over 3,700 pounds of hot iron that he was holding off the ground. While continuing to lift the Camaro, Boyle shouted for the driver that had hit Holtrust, who was watching in a complete daze from the side of the road, to come and help. "I yelled at him like four or five times, and then he finally reached underneath and pulled [Holtrust] out," Boyle told the *Arizona Daily Star.* "The driver must've been in shock, and he couldn't seem to come out of it."

When Holtrust was finally pulled out from underneath the car, he was in bad shape, but he was conscious and alive. Within a few minutes, an ambulance arrived and Holtrust was rushed to a nearby hospital. When he got there, he was treated for severe head and leg injuries. Holtrust would require months of rehab, but he would survive. Given the circumstances, that was nothing short of a miracle.

Although Boyle had more than tripled the world-record deadlift—the record is 1,102 pounds; a Camaro weighs about 3,700 pounds—he wasn't about to start training for Olympic powerlifting. He simply returned to work the next day as a paint shop supervisor. Outside of his transformation into the Incredible Hulk for those few heroic moments, Boyle was a regular guy.

This story is incredible, but there are others just like it. These unbelievable exhibitions of strength are so common that the scientific community recognizes these acts of "superhuman" and "hysterical" strength as being very real. Acts of superhuman strength almost always occur in life-or-death situations. According to J. Javier Provencio, MD, director of the neurological intensive care unit (ICU) at the Cleveland Clinic, in ordinary circumstances the body shuts down well in advance of its limits. Fear, fatigue, and pain act as protective mechanisms. These sensations signal to us that if we continue with an enormous challenge, there is a good chance we'll fail or injure ourselves. So we stop. But in extraordinary situations, like when someone's life is on the line, we are capable of overriding these defenses. We no longer feel fear, fatigue, or pain. As a result, we can push ourselves closer to our actual limits (like lifting a Camaro). If someone had asked Boyle to lift a Camaro on a regular Sunday afternoon he probably would have laughed and not even tried. Even if he were offered thousands of dollars for lifting the car, Boyle wouldn't have been able to do it. His mind would have shut down his body. Boyle was only able to lift the car because Holtrust was being crushed underneath it.

But what if there were a way to harness the source of this unbelievable strength in our own lives, and to draw upon it regularly? A University of Michigan public health professor named Victor Strecher, PhD, says that we can. Strecher knows this not just from his research but also from his own life. He is someone with firsthand experience when it comes to emerging from underneath the heaviest of weights.

BREAKING THROUGH THE LIMITS OF YOUR"SELF"

Strecher is a living legend around Ann Arbor, Michigan. He is a highly decorated professor, an expert on health behavior change, and a successful entrepreneur, having sold his locally developed health technology firm to a multibillion-dollar conglomerate in 2008. But perhaps more than anything, Strecher is known for his energy and enthusiasm in the classroom. Watching him teach is like watching performance art, only he's not putting on a show. He is fully engaged with his students and his passion is evident. The energy he brings to the lecture hall is palpable.

In 2010, when Brad was preparing to begin graduate school at the University of Michigan, everyone told him to take Strecher's course. It didn't matter that Brad was not studying health behavior change and communication, the subject Strecher taught. "Just get into the room with Strecher," Brad recalls his faculty advisor, an economist, telling him. "Good things will happen for your brain." Unfortunately, when Brad went to sign up for Strecher's class, he noticed that Strecher wouldn't be teaching that semester.

STRECHER AND HIS FAMILY were on vacation in the Dominican Republic in the spring of 2010. The weather was perfect. He was surrounded by his wife, his daughters, and their boyfriends. If anyone knows the importance of relishing in these kinds of good times with loved ones, it's Strecher. The man had learned to take nothing for granted.

When the younger of his two daughters, Julia, was just 14 months old, she contracted a horrific case of chickenpox. The virus spread rampantly and attacked her heart, which quickly began to fail. Julia's health declined fast, and her life hung in the balance. She needed a miracle, and she got one. On Valentine's Day 1991, at the University of North Carolina Medical Center, Julia underwent one of the first pediatric heart transplants ever. It worked. Julia survived.

Fast-forward 8 years and Julia, then age 9, became sick again. Although Strecher and his wife, Jeri, tried not to get overly nervous with every little scare (though who could blame them for doing so?) they sensed something was very wrong with their daughter. Their intuition was right. They took her to the doctor and were confronted with the worst possible news: Her second heart was failing. She needed another miracle, another heart. For the Strechers, it was back to the pediatric ICU and the sleepless nights that accompany it.

Julia received another heart, but this time around the transplant was followed by dire complications. Strecher thought his daughter was going to die. He remembers his wife, Jeri, even in this horrific moment, being the ultimate giver. "Jeri was making sure there was a plan to extract and donate Julia's organs," he told us. "We really thought this was the end." But lo and behold, Julia came around. Strecher says no one could really explain it then, and he still can't explain it now. It was another miracle.

Julia grew into a smart and beautiful young lady. She was finishing her first year of nursing school when she and her boyfriend joined her family in the Dominican Republic for spring break. Everything was wonderful—until it wasn't. On March 2, 2010, Julia's heart suddenly stopped beating. This time, neither this heart nor any other one placed inside her chest would ever start beating again. At age 19, with what should have been a full life ahead of her, Julia was dead.

One broken heart led to another. Strecher retreated into a very dark place, suffering in a way that only someone who has lost a child can understand. After her second heart transplant, well aware that Julia's life was truly a blessing, Strecher made it his purpose to help his daughter lead a big and fulfilled life. They traveled the world together, rode elephants in Northern Thailand and went paragliding in the Rocky Mountains, jumping off a 30-foot-tall boulder into a pool of water. But that purpose died with Julia. "I just didn't care about living at all," recalls Strecher. "I'd lost my way."

Three months after Julia passed away, Strecher withdrew, alone, to a remote cabin in Northern Michigan. One early morning, after dreaming about Julia, Strecher paddled a kayak out into the middle of a lake. It was only 5 a.m. The sun was rising, and aside from the small waves rippling off his boat, Strecher was surrounded by nothing but still water. "I just started sobbing out there, and I felt Julia come into me," he recalls. "She said, 'You've got to move forward, Dad.'"

Strecher would later realize this occurred on Father's Day.

AT THAT MOMENT, Strecher recognized how empty he was. He told us that Julia was speaking to him, making him realize that he couldn't go on living like this—without a "why." He needed to renew his purpose. Then he had an epiphany. He thought that perhaps as he rekindled his own purpose he could help others find theirs. He felt strongly that Julia was telling him to take this path.

Clinging on to this message from his daughter, Strecher wasted no time. He shifted much of his research to understanding the power of purpose. He also began teaching again. As you can imagine, this wasn't easy. "I saw Julia's face in every student," he says. As time passed, Strecher committed to developing new purposes in his own life. One of them would be "to teach every one of my students as if they were my own daughter."

Then something remarkable happened. Strecher started to feel better.

He still hurt, but he emerged from the dark place he was in. By no means was his progress immediate, but he began to feel better about waking up each day. He started to enjoy living again. And in a fascinating confluence of events, his research was helping to explain the transformation he was experiencing.

Strecher discovered that throughout history, when people focus on a self-transcending purpose, or a purpose greater than themselves, they become capable of more than they ever thought was possible. Strecher believes this is because when we concentrate

When we transcend our "self" and minimize our ego, a whole new realm of possibilities emerges.

deeply on something beyond ourselves, our ego is minimized. A large part of our ego's role is to literally protect our "self." It is our ego that tells us to shut down and flee when faced with threats. When we transcend our "self" and minimize our ego, however, we can overcome the fears, anxieties, and physiological protective mechanisms that so often hold us back from achieving major breakthroughs. A whole new realm of possibilities emerges.

By focusing on helping others and teaching his students as if they were his own daughter, Strecher was able to overcome the loss of Julia. By focusing on saving Kyle Holtrust's life, Boyle was able to lift a 3,700-pound car. Although these stories may seem different at first blush, they are both examples of how individuals channeling a self-transcending purpose can overcome pain, fear, and fatigue to accomplish something that seems impossible.

In order to more fully understand how this phenomenon works, it is instructive to turn to an unlikely place: exercise science.

IS FATIGUE ALL IN YOUR HEAD?

In the early 1990s, in a physiology lab at the University of Cape Town in South Africa, an exercise scientist named Tim Noakes, MD, unveiled a radical new way to think about fatigue. Until then, prevailing wisdom held that fatigue occurred in the body. At a certain intensity or duration of physical effort, the demands we put on our muscles become too great and, eventually, our muscles fail. Ask any athlete, from a marathon runner to a powerlifter, and they will be familiar with the feeling. It's not a particularly comfortable one. What at first is a manageable burn becomes worse and worse until they can no longer bear it. The runner's pace slows to a mere shuffle; the powerlifter can't manage to hoist the barbell up for one last rep. Try as they might, they simply run out of gas and their muscles cease to contract.

Noakes, however, wasn't convinced that fatigue occurred in the body or that muscles actually ran out of gas. He questioned why so many athletes, seemingly overwhelmed by fatigue, were suddenly able to speed up during the final stretch of a race when the end was in sight. If the muscles were truly dead, Noakes hypothesized, these finish-line spurts would be impossible. To prove his point, Noakes attached electrical sensors to athletes and then instructed them to lift weights with their legs until they simply couldn't lift any longer. (In exercise science, this is called "inducing muscle failure.") When the weights slammed down and each participant tapped out, reporting they could no longer contract their muscles, Noakes ran an electrical current through the sensor. Much to the surprise of everyone—especially to the participants whose legs were dead— their muscles contracted. Although the participants could not contract their muscles on their own, Noakes proved that their muscles actually had more to give. The participants felt drained, but empirically, their muscles were not.

Noakes repeated similar versions of this experiment and observed the same result. Although participants reported being totally depleted and unable to contract their muscles after exercising to what they *thought* was failure, when electrical stimulation was applied, without fail, their muscles produced additional force. This led Noakes to conclude that contrary to popular belief, physical fatigue occurs not in the body, but in the brain. It's not that our muscles wear out; rather, it is our brain that shuts them down when they still have a few more percentage points to give. Noakes speculates this is an innately programmed way of protecting ourselves. Physiologically, we could push our bodies to true failure (i.e., injury and organ failure), but the brain comes in and creates a perception of failure before we actually harm ourselves. The brain, Noakes remarked, is our "central governor" of fatigue. It's our "ego" shutting us down when confronted by fear and threat. In other words, we are hardwired to retreat when the going gets tough. But like Boyle and Strecher demonstrated, it is possible to override the central governor.

PURPOSE AND OVERRIDING
THE CENTRAL GOVERNOR

The Appalachian Trail (AT) runs 2,185 miles from Springer Mountain in Georgia to Mount Katahdin in Maine. It takes most people between 5 and 7 months to hike the AT in its entirety. But in 2011, a young woman named Jennifer Pharr Davis was trying to break the speed record by finishing the hike in less than 50 days.

Unfortunately, by the 12th day of her record-attempting hike, with over 1,650 miles remaining, Pharr Davis was broken down, depleted, and ready to give up. Perhaps the most disabling combination for a hiker—shin splints and diarrhea—had been wreaking havoc on her body for the past 4 days. Negative thoughts and fear were poisoning her mind. "It was the perfect storm," Pharr Davis told us. "I was already way off pace and thought, 'There is no way I can get the record.' I gave up." She approached a juncture on New Hampshire roads where she was meeting her husband, Brew, who was supporting the hike. She was sad to quit, but relieved to be done.

The buildup to that juncture started 7 years earlier when Pharr Davis was 21. Upon finishing college, it struck her that her traditional education had "happened in a box." She knew nothing about the natural environment, and sensed that something central to her human experience was missing. Though she wasn't completely sure why, she longed to connect with nature.

So, upon graduating college in 2005, Pharr Davis set out on the AT for the first time. The experience taught her far more than rudimentary backpacking skills. "I met wonderful companions and felt indescribable awe," she said. "I learned to prioritize people and experiences over stuff." But perhaps more than anything, she connected with nature in a visceral way. "I discovered nature was not separate from me, but that I could be a part of nature, flowing with it." Pharr Davis said she felt closest to God while on the trail. "I realized that maybe my gift is an ability to move swiftly in the wilderness. As a Christian, I felt obligated to use that gift."

And use that gift she did. Pharr Davis became an avid hiker and spent an increasing proportion of her waking hours out in nature. Just a few years later, in 2008, with more training under her belt and the support (both on and off the trail) of her new husband, Pharr Davis hiked the AT in 57 days. It marked the fastest-known time ever for a woman. By then, hiking had become an integral part of her life. She started to think, "Maybe I could break the overall record."

The overall record stood at 47½ days and had been held by a long line of competitive male athletes who specialized in ultra-endurance events. Although Pharr Davis's breaking the overall record would be akin to a woman beating all the professional men at the Boston Marathon (i.e., unthinkable), she had unshakeable self-belief and the backing of her husband Brew. They devoted themselves to going for it, dedicating the next 3 years of their lives to training and preparation.

Fast-forward to June 28, 2011, when Pharr Davis's drive and chances of breaking the overall record came to a crippling halt as she approached Brew on those New Hampshire roads. "I finally got to Brew and told him I was quitting," she says, but "Brew was not okay with it." Brew, who was supporting the record attempt, reminded her that he had given up so much of himself for her, and that this was a team effort. It was only then, looking into her husband's eyes, that she realized something critical. "Until then, everything had been about me and the record," she said. "I was a slave to the record; it was all I was thinking about." At that moment, though, Pharr Davis had a revelation that changed everything:

I just totally released from the record. I started hiking out of a greater faith. I wanted to honor my God, to get back to the reasons that got me hooked on hiking to begin with—a love for the wilderness, a love for my husband, and to use my gift. I remembered that I feel closest to God when I am hiking up and down the trail as a part of nature, when I am loving my husband, when I am relishing in my gift. All of a sudden, the hike was no longer about a record, it was no longer about me. The whole thing became an act of worship to something greater than myself.

Although her physical discomfort ebbed and flowed throughout the hike, Pharr Davis's psychological distress evaporated after that paradigm shift. Once she stopped focusing on herself and instead became absorbed in thoughts that were beyond herself, she quickly ascended from the deep hole she was in. She felt renewed, refreshed, and reenergized. She told us her fatigue eased and she became more comfortable confronting her fears. With her mind rapt in love for her husband, love for nature, and love for her god, she hiked on.

Thirty-four days later, after averaging over 47 miles per day on the gnarliest terrain, Pharr Davis had accomplished the impossible. She shattered the overall record by 26 hours, a feat that earned her the title of National Geographic Adventurer of the Year.*

WHEN WE SHARED PHARR DAVIS'S STORY with Strecher, the University of Michigan professor who studies purpose, he responded with an unusually short email: "Wow." He later told us Pharr Davis's experience on the Appalachian Trail is a profound example of ego minimization. He explained that she was harnessing the power of purpose to overcome her fears and

---

* In the spring of 2016, an ultra-endurance athlete named Karl Meltzer set a new record of 45 days and 22 hours. Interestingly, when Brad interviewed Meltzer for *Runner's World* magazine, he said that whenever he found himself in darks spots, he would show gratitude to those supporting him and immediately feel better. The less Meltzer thought about himself, the better he performed.

doubts, and pointed us to new brain science that sheds light on what may have been unfolding inside her head.

For a recent study published in the *Proceedings of the National Academy of Sciences*, researchers, including Strecher, used fMRI scans to examine what happens inside the brain when people are presented with threatening messages. Individuals who were asked to reflect deeply on their core values prior to receiving a threatening message showed heightened neural activity in a part of the brain associated with "positive valuation." In other words, their underlying neurology became more receptive to an otherwise threatening situation. They were overriding their central governor. Instead of shutting them down when faced with a threat, their brains were moving them toward the challenge. What's more, these effects were not confined solely to the lab. The individuals who reflected on their core values actually went on to overcome threats and fears in their lives at a much greater rate than a control group.

What Pharr Davis accomplished physically on the AT is extraordinary, and undoubtedly requires a gift that lies at least partially in genetics. But what she did psychologically is no less remarkable, and is accessible to all of us. By focusing on something beyond ourselves and reflecting on our core values, we can all more courageously confront challenges and improve our performance.

It's not just physical performance that improves with a self-transcending purpose. In a meta-analysis of over 200,000 workers (nonathletes) across numerous industries, researchers found the belief that one's job had a positive impact on others was associated with better performance. Other research suggests that purpose reduces burnout and even helps with adherence to challenging health behaviors like dieting or quitting smoking. All of this makes sense. In situations that feel scary or overwhelming, our brain—our central governor, our ego, our "self"—automatically tries to protect us from failure. It shuts

> *By focusing on something beyond ourselves and reflecting on our core values, we can all more courageously confront challenges and improve our performance.*

PERFORMANCE PRACTICES

- Our "ego" or "self" or "central governor" serves as a protective mechanism that holds us back from reaching our true limits.

- When faced with great challenges, our ego is biologically programmed to shut us down, telling us to turn in the other direction.

- By focusing on a self-transcending purpose, or a reason for doing something beyond our "self," we can override our ego and break through our self-imposed limits.

- To the extent you can, link your activities to a greater purpose (more on how to do this in Chapter 9). This way, when you are faced with formidable challenges and your mind is telling you to quit, you can ask yourself why you are undertaking them. If the answer is "for someone or something greater than myself," you'll be more likely to push onward.

- Thinking less about your "self" is one of the best ways to improve yourself.

us down and tells us to turn in the other direction. Even if failure doesn't mean physical injury, our ego doesn't like emotional injury, either—it doesn't want to risk getting embarrassed, so it ushers us down the safe route. It's only when we transcend our "self" that we can break through our self-imposed limits.

In a paradoxical twist, the less we think about ourselves, the better we become.

PURPOSE AND MOTIVATION

A self-transcending purpose not only allows us to overcome our greatest fears and break through our limits, it also improves our performance in less heroic, everyday activities. In one study, researchers from the Wharton

School at the University of Pennsylvania found that hospital janitors who cleaned bedpans and mopped floors performed better and reported higher levels of satisfaction when their job was framed as being integral to the healing of other people. The janitors were constantly reminded that by keeping the hospital clean, they were minimizing the chance of bacteria spreading and harming the already vulnerable patients. They no longer saw their job as just removing vomit from the floors; they saw it as saving lives. Some hospitals have even eliminated the job titles "janitor" and "custodian" in favor of titles like "health and safety team member" or "environmental health worker."

Other research shows that college students working as phone solicitors asking alumni for donations improved their performance after a recent graduate spoke to them about how grateful he was for their work. This wasn't just any graduate student, though; he had attended the university on scholarship dollars raised via the solicitation efforts of the students. In the month following this meeting, the student solicitors raised 171 percent more money.

These are just two of many examples that show how linking one's work to a greater purpose enhances everyday performance, even on mundane tasks. Just ask yourself: Are you more likely to give something your all if you know doing so will benefit someone else or a greater cause? For almost every great performer we asked, the answer was an enthusiastic yes.

To learn more about why this is the case, much like we did to see how purpose helps us overcome our fears, we decided to yet again break down disciplinary barriers and turn to exercise science.

Samuele Marcora, PhD, is the director of research at the University of Kent School of Sport and Exercise Sciences. Like Noakes, Marcora believes that fatigue has both physical and psychological components. But unlike Noakes, Marcora thinks fatigue is more complicated than a protective central governor that only shuts

> *Just ask yourself: Are you more likely to give something your all if you know doing so will benefit someone else or a greater cause? For almost every great performer we asked, the answer was an enthusiastic yes.*

us down when we approach our limits. Instead, Marcora believes that we constantly weigh our perceptions of effort associated with an activity (i.e., how hard something feels) against our motivation to do that activity. When perception of effort is greater than motivation, we slow down or ease up until the two are balanced. It follows that the more motivated we are, the greater the perception of effort we are willing to tolerate. According to Marcora, an athlete can improve her performance by either decreasing her perception of effort (i.e., training her body so that running 5-minute miles *feels* easier) or by increasing her motivation.

When it comes to increasing motivation, a wide body of research suggests doing something for others is far more effective than traditional incentives like money or reputation. Perhaps this is why after unbelievable, record-breaking performances—ones that inevitably required enduring immense pain and suffering—athletes never say they were thinking about how great it would feel to be a champion or how much money they would win. Rather, after crossing the finish line, they almost always report that when the pain came on, they began thinking about their family, their god, or their friend who has cancer. They were able to endure the pain, to say "more" when their bodies were screaming "less," because they were supremely motivated by a self-transcending purpose.

One of our favorite examples is Ashton Eaton, the two-time Olympic champion decathlete who some say is the greatest athlete of all time. In order to break the world record at the 2015 world championships, Eaton needed to run faster than 4 minutes and 18 seconds in the final event, the 1500 meters. This posed a significant challenge in and of itself. But Eaton had already completed the other 9 events, and he had more or less locked up a gold medal. In other words, he was dead-tired and had little to gain from going all out, especially because the record he would be trying to break was his own, set a few years prior.

Nevertheless, Eaton decided to go for it. Why, you might wonder? Eaton told the media that when the pain came on, "I was just thinking, it's not for me so I have to go." When further questioned, Eaton said, "Really I was just thinking about me sitting on the couch when I was little and watching somebody like Michael Johnson or Carl Lewis jump and run, and that's the reason I'm here today. I thought maybe there's a kid on a couch somewhere and if I break this world record they may be inspired to do something." Eaton ran the 1500 in 4 minutes and 17 seconds.

Another example is Meb Keflezighi, who, in 2014, became the first American to win the Boston Marathon in over 30 years. His historic win was extra special because it occurred just 1 year after the horrific terrorist attack at the 2013 race. Keflezighi credits his incredible performance to the inspiration he felt while running for those who had died in the terrorist attack the year before (known as the Boston Bombing). He even wrote their names on his race bib. Representing both the victims of the prior year's attack, but also as the top American in the race, he ran with greater purpose and motivation. "Toward the end I was remembering the victims who passed away," he said. "They helped carry me through."

While Marcora's research and the examples of Eaton and Keflezighi are in the realm of athletics, it's easy to see this theory come to life in other arenas, too. By linking their work to a greater purpose, for example, the hospital

Purpose fosters motivation; motivation lets us endure a greater perception of effort; and enduring a greater perception of effort often results in better performance.

janitors and student solicitors increased their motivation in a big way. As a result, they were able to tolerate a greater perceived effort on the job, whether this meant cleaning more arduously or calling more alumni with heightened focus and engagement. Ultimately, they performed better.

Purpose fosters motivation; motivation lets us endure a greater perception of effort; and enduring a greater perception of effort often results in better performance. This equation holds true in every field—from the track to the workplace. And as we're about to see, it even holds true in the artist's studio.

EMIL ALZAMORA HAS ART in his DNA. Both his mother and grandmother were successful artists. He grew up in Lima, Peru, just a short walk from the ceramics studio where his family worked. He was drawing before he was walking. "Art was everywhere," he recalled. "I was totally immersed in it." Though he never felt pressured by his family to pursue art, he was naturally drawn to it. Eventually he moved to the United States, where he attended Florida State University College of Fine Arts, graduating magna cum laude. The only problem was that while his education left him technically sound on art theory and art history, he hadn't learned much about sculpting, the form he was most drawn to.

In order to gain the real-world experience he needed, he moved to New York City and began working at Polich Tallix, an internationally recognized foundry. There, he worked alongside some of the best sculptors in the world. "It took great stamina," he explains, "but for the first time, I was learning what it meant to be a sculptor." Alzamora learned fast, and he rose quickly in the art scene. It wasn't long before his works were being exhibited across the world at sites that included the United Nations building, PepsiCo's world headquarters, and the Queens Museum. He has also received positive reviews from numerous publications, including the prestigious *New York Times* arts section. But while the acclaim and praise is great, for Alzamora the work that lay underneath it is even greater. "I feel like an endurance athlete," Alzamora told us. "My approach to sculpture is a physical tribulation. A constant battle against fatigue."

Yet the physical demands are minor when Alzamora considers his duty to his family. Trying to make a career out of art is risky business. There is no job security, nor are there any guarantees. The artist is subject to the whims of the gallery owner, critic, and collector, and dramatic ups and downs are common. Though it takes years of hard work, risk, and delayed income to even have a chance of making it to the top of the art world, once there, it can feel like an arduous battle to remain. As we mentioned in the Introduction of this book, anxiety and even depression are highly prevalent in artists, and Alzamora admitted his anxiety to us. But he told us that when he wakes up in the morning, his "mission to promote growth and positivity through my art trumps my anxiety."

"It's a real struggle to deal with all the non-art parts of the art world,"

Alzamora says. "It can be a vicious environment rife with politics and back-stabbing." He went on to tell us that he often feels discouraged and worn out from all the business aspects of the industry: the "selling" not only of his work, but also of himself. "If it were up to me, I would wake up, eat break-fast, and make art all day, every day. Unfortunately, I can no longer do that."

Alzamora is a realist; he understands that he needs to make a living to support his family. But that doesn't make it any easier for him to endure everything peripheral to the art, all of which becomes more time- and energy-consuming as he becomes better known. He told us that when he is most fed up—on the verge of wanting to quit altogether—it's not the poten-tial financial rewards or the acclaim he'll receive for his next great work that he thinks about. "When I'm really down and drowning in it, I remind myself of *why* I do this in the first place," he said. "I create art to make peo-ple smile, cry, connect to one another, and connect to the earth. To be a part of something bigger. That makes putting up with all the crap worth it."

PURPOSE AND GRIT

University of Pennsylvania psychologist Angela Duckworth, PhD, might say that Alzamora is a particularly "gritty" artist. Duckworth won a MacArthur Fellowship "genius grant" for her work on "grit," or the ten-dency to sustain interest in and effort toward very long-term goals. Duck-worth says that grit is a "hallmark of high achievers in every domain." Gritty people hang in there and persevere when others quit.

Duckworth found that grit is not innate. Rather, it can be cultivated over time. While there is no single way to develop grit, the trait is often accompanied by a strong sense of purpose. Especially when the going gets tough, gritty people draw upon a greater cause for inspiration and stick-to-itiveness. As Duckworth and her colleagues wrote in a 2014 paper, "Highly aversive experiences may become more bearable when they are viewed as having positive

> *When the going gets tough, gritty people draw upon a greater cause for inspiration and stick-to-itiveness.*

consequences that transcend the self." The power of purpose strikes yet again, this time as a theme underlying grit.

Perhaps the most extreme example of grit can be seen in Holocaust survivors. Even after being starved and tortured, and watching their loved ones get shipped off to the gas chambers, Holocaust survivors continued fighting to live. While the horrors of the Holocaust are unimaginable for those of us who did not experience them, a psychiatrist and Holocaust survivor named Viktor Frankl, PhD, has shed light on how he and others managed to survive. In his book, *Man's Search for Meaning*, Frankl wrote, "A man who becomes conscious of the responsibility he bears toward a human being who affectionately waits for him, or to an unfinished work, will never be able to throw away his life."

Of course this is the most extreme example, and we are by no means attempting to equate enduring a tough stretch at the office or the gym to surviving the Holocaust. But we decided to include Frankl's insights because they exemplify, in quite a profound and extreme manner, how being motivated by a self-transcending purpose allows one to endure even the toughest—the most horrific—of situations.

PERFORMANCE PRACTICES

- We are constantly balancing perception of effort, or how hard something feels, with motivation.
- If we want to endure more effort, which often leads to better performance, we may need to increase our motivation.
- The best way to increase motivation is to link our work to a greater purpose or cause.
- Not only will focusing on activities that help others make the world a better place, it will also make you a better performer.
- Especially when we are feeling tired or worn out, we should think about *why* we are doing what we are doing.

GIVE BACK TO GET BACK

Burnout tends to strike at the worst times. If you're an athlete, you might be in, or on your way to, the best shape of your life. If you're a business person, perhaps you just landed a new promotion that you worked your ass off to get. If you're an artist, maybe you're nearing completion of your masterpiece. And then all of a sudden you just don't feel like doing it anymore. You lose the drive, passion, and interest. You burn out.

Burnout is intimately linked to our fight-or-flight stress response. After a prolonged period of too much stress, our "flight" trigger kicks in, urging us to flee from whatever it is that is causing the stress. Burnout is quite common in people who are pushing to get the most out of themselves. This is because continually growing and improving requires adding stress over days, weeks, months, and years. As we discussed in Section 1 of this book, alternating between periods of stress and rest helps prevent burnout. Even so, when we push close to our breaking point (and remember, that's the goal) we run the risk of pushing just a bit too hard and crossing a fine line. When this happens, we start feeling burnt out.

Traditional thinking on burnout advises that we take an extended break from our work, whatever that work might be. Sometimes this can be effective, but often it's not an option. An Olympic hopeful can't just stop training 6 months out from a qualifying event, and most people can't just take 3 months off from their jobs. Not to mention, when people do completely remove themselves from whatever endeavor led to their burnout, many lose their connection and never return.

The good news is that behavioral science offers an alternative approach for managing burnout that does not require extended time off and has the potential to actually strengthen your drive and motivation. We are going to call this "give back to get back," and it's based on the research of psychology professors Shelley Taylor, PhD, of the University of California, Los Angeles, and Adam Grant, PhD, of the Wharton School at the University of Pennsylvania. The basic premise of "give back to get back" is that instead of moving away from your work when burnout strikes, you may actually need to move closer to it, albeit in a different manner.

Giving back is a powerful antidote to burnout.

That different manner is "giving back" to your field. This can take many forms, including volunteering and mentoring, but the basic gist is that you should focus on helping others. Helping others activates reward and pleasure centers in the brain. Not only does this make you feel better, but it also helps you re-associate positive emotions with your pursuit. For these reasons, giving back often results in renewed energy and motivation. In his *New York Times* bestselling book *Give and Take*, Grant references research from across fields—from teaching to nursing—to show that giving back is a powerful antidote to burnout.

But aren't teaching and nursing inherently helping fields? In theory, yes, which is why they attract people who are naturally inclined to give in the first place. But as any teacher or nurse will tell you, in the day-to-day grind of the work, it's very easy to lose sight of direct student/patient impact and instead feel like a small cog in an inefficient machine. This is why providing opportunities for teachers and nurses to directly help others in a manner that yields tangible results has been proven to reduce burnout. Grant writes that having a "sense of lasting impact protect[s] against stress, preventing exhaustion," and he encourages people in high-stress jobs to actively seek out opportunities to "give back" in intimate ways.

While we could go on forever about Grant's compelling research on the powers of giving back, his personal story is equally as telling. Long before becoming a bestselling author and one of the country's top-rated professors, Grant was a competitive diver, twice earning high school All-America honors before diving collegiately at Harvard.

During our discussion on "giving," Grant reflected back to his senior year of high school, when he confronted a serious case of burnout himself. "Back then," he told us, "diving was my life. I practiced 9 hours a day the summer between my junior and senior years, so much that I kept duct tape on the bottom of my feet as a second layer of skin to manage [the] blisters [I got] from scraping against the board all day." Grant's training had gone even better than expected, and he was in a great place heading into the biggest meet of his senior year. He was in the best form of his life—he told us that he "was ready for a peak performance." And then Grant had an off-day. What should have been the climax to 4 years of hard work and dedication turned out to be a total disaster. He missed his dives and got beaten by a bunch of athletes who he had beaten easily before. "I went to a dark place," Grant said. "I was depressed, and I didn't want to touch a diving board again."

In Grant's mind, he was done with the sport, and he no longer wanted to dive collegiately. But others in the diving community could not bear to see his career end that way, especially when his best years were still ahead of him. After tons of tough love, Grant's mentors finally convinced him to come back to the pool. Not as an athlete, but as a coach of younger divers. "It completely rejuvenated me," Grant said of coaching. "I took a tremendous amount of joy in working with and seeing other divers get better. It reminded me what I loved about diving in the first place—how much personal growth I experienced through the sport." It wasn't long after getting into coaching that Grant was back on the board himself, going on to have a successful collegiate diving career.

Grant's story especially resonated with one of us. As you read earlier, Steve was beyond burnt out from running. There was a period when Steve wanted nothing to do with the sport that he had given so much of the first 22 years of his life to. But it wasn't an extended break or sports psychology that brought Steve back into the running community. Rather, it was coaching. Long before Steve was a coach of Olympians, he started coaching high school runners.

Much like Grant did with coaching divers, Steve found fulfillment in volunteering to help coach a raggedy team of teenage runners who were in need of mentorship. At the time, Steve was heartbroken that he couldn't run a mile in under 4 minutes. But then he saw how thrilled the kids he coached were to run a mile in under 6 minutes and he couldn't help but smile. Moments like these reminded Steve of what the sport was all about: fair competition and the simple act of working hard to improve oneself. By shifting his focus away from trying to be America's best runner and toward helping others, Steve slowly but surely regained his love for the sport.

PERFORMANCE PRACTICES

- Find opportunities to give back in the context of your work; these can be more intensive, such as coaching and mentoring, or less intensive, such as posting sincere advice in online forums.

- The only criteria is that your "giving" is closely linked to your work and that you give without the expectation of getting anything back.

- While "giving" is especially powerful for preventing and reversing burnout, you should still aim to avoid burnout by supporting stress with appropriate rest.

THE POWER OF PURPOSE

While some may possess a self-transcending purpose, others may not. And the idea that one can simply come up with a self-transcending purpose out of thin air seems like a fool's errand. But a self-transcending purpose doesn't come from thin air. It comes from inside you. You just have to find it. University of Michigan professor Strecher has created a tool that helps individuals create their own self-transcending purposes based on their core values. Using Strecher's step-by-step process, we came up with the following purpose for writing this book:

> *Help people discover how they can get the most out of themselves in a healthy and sustainable way, and prevent the next case of burnout, dissatisfaction, and unhappiness.*

We've referenced this purpose throughout the process of writing this book and reflected upon it regularly, especially at times when we were discouraged, scared, or downright tired.

In the next chapter, we'll walk you through the process of developing your own self-transcending purpose (and reaffirming it if you already have one), and then recommend some of the best ways that you can harness it.

But first, to reiterate the power of purpose, we'll leave you with the following words from Holocaust survivor and psychiatrist Victor Frankl:

> By declaring that man is responsible and must actualize the potential meaning of his life, I wish to stress that the true meaning of life is to be discovered in the world rather than within man or his own psyche, as though it were a closed system. I have termed this constitutive characteristic "the self-transcendence of human existence." It denotes the fact that being human always points, and is directed, to something or someone, other than oneself—be it a meaning to fulfill or another human being to encounter. The more one forgets himself—by giving himself to a cause to serve or another person to love—the more human he is and the more he actualizes himself. What is called self-actualization is not an attainable aim at all, for the simple reason that the more one would strive for it, the more he would miss it. In other words, self-actualization is possible only as a side-effect of self-transcendence.

DEVELOP YOUR PURPOSE

In this chapter, you'll develop your purpose.* If you already have one, consider this an opportunity to fine-tune and reaffirm it. After homing in on your purpose, you'll learn some simple ways to weave it into your day, ensuring that you live in alignment with it and harness its performance-enhancing power. But before we dive right in, it is important to dispel a few common misconceptions.

- You need not be religious, or even spiritual, to have a purpose.

- Purpose isn't a mystical endeavor. As you are about to find out, the process of creating a purpose is based upon rational reflection.

---

* This process is inspired by the original On Purpose mobile application developed by Victor Strecher, PhD. We thank Strecher not only for helping us find our purpose, but also for giving us permission to use his process to help you find yours. For more on Strecher's approach, visit www.JoolHealth.com.

- It's okay to have more than one purpose. For example, in the previous chapter we shared with you our purpose for writing this book, but we also have additional purposes that apply to other areas of our lives.

- It's also okay to have only one purpose. Some people have one purpose that cuts across everything they do. For example:

  - To serve and honor my god by being the best person I can be every day.

  - To bring positive energy to everything I do and to share that energy with everyone I interact with.

  - To pause and reflect on how my actions (prior to acting) will impact others.

- No one is stopping you from having a *self-centered* purpose. But as you read in the previous chapter, self-transcending purposes not only make the world a better place, they also enhance your performance. So while it's not a requirement, we encourage you to find ways to apply your strengths to something greater than yourself.

- Your purpose can change over time. As a matter of fact, it should! Perhaps the only constant in life is change. Revisit this process as often as you like.

Developing an initial draft of your purpose should take about 15 to 20 minutes, and we suggest doing it in one sitting. While we strongly recommend everyone go through this process,* if you are certain you've already honed your purpose, you can skip ahead to page 185 where we discuss how you can best harness its performance-enhancing power.

---

* Admittedly, we (i.e., Brad and Steve) don't love it when books include activities like this. But we guarantee this one is worthwhile.

SELECT YOUR CORE VALUES

Core values are your fundamental beliefs and guiding principles. They are the things that matter most to you, and they help dictate your behavior and actions. Select up to five core values from the list that follows. This list isn't comprehensive, so if something comes to mind that you don't see here, go ahead and use it.

- Achievement
- Commitment
- Community
- Consistency
- Courage
- Creativity
- Education
- Efficiency
- Enjoyment
- Enthusiasm
- Expertise
- Honesty
- Independence
- Inspiration
- Kindness
- Loyalty
- Motivation
- Optimism
- Positivity
- Pragmatism
- Relationships
- Responsibility
- Security
- Self-control
- Spirituality
- Tradition
- Reliability
- Reputation
- Vitality

For example, when developing our purpose for writing this book we selected the following core values:

- Community
- Creativity
- Enjoyment
- Expertise
- Relationships

PERSONALIZE YOUR CORE VALUES

For each core value that you selected, write a sentence or two that "customizes" it, making it more personal to you. Here is how we customized the core values underlying our decision to write this book:

- **Community:** Help readers get more out of themselves and enjoy the process of doing so.

- **Creativity:** Unify disparate ideas from across domains in a way that is meaningful and insightful.

- **Enjoyment:** Have fun! We love to learn, and we love the challenge of communicating, so we should keep that in mind and relish in it! If we enjoy the process of writing, we're likely to do a better job at it.

- **Expertise:** Gain knowledge in a subject area that we are both passionate about: health and human performance. Apply what we learn in our own lives and share this knowledge with readers so they, too, can apply it in theirs.

- **Relationships:** Take advantage of this opportunity to develop relationships with interesting people whom we can continue to interact with and learn from, well beyond the process of writing this book.

RANK YOUR CORE VALUES

Here comes the hard part. Now that you've personalized your core values, rank them, with the first being the most deeply held value (i.e., the most important). For example, our ranking looks like this:

1. Creativity

2. Community

3. Relationships

4. Expertise

5. Enjoyment

WRITE YOUR PURPOSE STATEMENT

Congratulations. You've selected and reflected upon your core values. Now you are primed to write your purpose statement. Your purpose statement should reflect your customized core values and should be anywhere from one to three sentences. Here are a few examples:

- Help people discover how they can get the most out of themselves in a healthy and sustainable way, and prevent the next case of burnout, dissatisfaction, and unhappiness.

- Be ready for someone when they need me—because I've had so much help and love from other people when I needed them!

- Give the children in my school a clean building.

- Study and understand nature, then give this knowledge to others.

- Be more engaged with my partner.

- Be the best athlete that I can be so that others are inspired to push their own limits.

- Make beautiful art that makes people smile, cry, connect to one another, and connect to the earth.

HARNESSING THE POWER OF YOUR PURPOSE

We hope that you found the process for developing a purpose as valuable as we did. It's okay if you aren't certain that you came up with the perfect purpose. As a matter of fact, even if you feel like you did, we encourage you to revisit your purpose (and the process that led you to it) the next time you pick up this book. Refinement is always encouraged, especially early on.

Soon enough, however, you should feel comfortable that your purpose is accurate—that is to say, it reflects who you are and what you believe in.

Now it's time to put your purpose to use. What follows are practical ways for you to systematically remind yourself of your purpose and harness its power. As you're about to read, nothing that we suggest is too hard or time-consuming. In total, these tips should add no more than 3 minutes to your day. But these simple ways to weave purpose into your life pay large dividends. They are designed to make you a healthier, happier, and better person. And while that last sentence sounds like it's born out of the self-help canon, you'll soon see that it's actually born out of science.

Visual Cues

Write down your purpose and strategically stick it in places where you are likely to need a boost. This way, when the going gets tough, your purpose is right there to remind you *why* you are working so hard. As we discussed in the previous chapter, research shows that reflecting on your core values and purpose literally changes your brain in ways conducive to overcoming fear and increasing motivation and grit. Even if you only glance at your purpose for a split second, perhaps not even fully processing it, simply having it within your visual field can help. Studies show that non-conscious visual cues (i.e., those that we don't fully process) can alter the perception of effort, making something that is objectively hard feel easier. And as we mentioned in the previous chapter, consciously engaging with your purpose, even for just a few seconds, can have profound effects on your brain and subsequent motivation.

> *Write down your purpose and strategically stick it in places where you are likely to need a boost.*

Here are a few examples of how great performers strategically use visual cues to remind themselves of their purpose when they are likely to need it most:

- A professional bike racer puts his purpose on the handlebars of his bike. Whenever the pace, and associated pain, picks up, his natural inclination is to drop his head and look down. Every time he does that, he'll be looking at his purpose: *To inspire other people to get out of their comfort zones and live life to its fullest.* And then, he'll proceed to push a bit harder and endure a bit more suffering.

- A middle manager at a health care company often gets frustrated when frontline staff call her with what she thinks are stupid questions about a report her department publishes. She notices herself being short on the phone and, at times, even ignoring calls altogether. She writes her job-specific purpose—*to make a difference in the lives of other human beings*—on a sticky note that she sticks to her phone. This way, whenever the phone rings, she connects questions about the report, however trivial they may seem, to the report's ultimate purpose: improving patient care. Now, every time the phone rings, she'll be reminded that providing a thoughtful and correct answer is an input to helping sick people heal, to *making a difference in the lives of other people.*

- An artist created a word-art version of her purpose and blew it up. But she didn't post this in the studio. She posted it in her office. As you heard earlier, the hardest part about the job for many artists is all the non-art stuff. Having her purpose in her office reminds her of why she puts up with the all the extraneous crap—*so she can make beautiful art that moves people.*

- We (Steve and Brad) put our purpose on our computers! Whenever we sat down to write, we were reminded of why we were working. We are confident that you are reading a better book because of this. As a matter of fact, without our purpose, we aren't even sure if we would have written this book to begin with. Going part-time in our more traditional jobs to write a book was scary. Our prior setup was much safer financially, but we weren't *helping people discover how they can get the most out of themselves in a healthy and sustainable way, and preventing the next case of burnout, dissatisfaction, and unhappiness.* This little reminder gave us the courage and confidence to write on.

Hopefully these examples can help you think of the perfect places to tag with your purpose: places where you may need a little extra courage to overcome fear or a boost in motivation to endure. The key is that your purpose is somewhere that you're likely to look during challenges. We also recommend sticking your purpose on your bathroom mirror. This serves as a nice way to mark the start of your day and helps you get the most out of it.

Self-Talk

Merriam-Webster's dictionary defines "mantra" in a few ways. The most common definition is "a word or phrase that is repeated often or that expresses someone's basic beliefs." The other definition is "a mystical formula of invocation." An invocation, meanwhile, is defined as "the action of invoking something or someone for assistance; the summoning of the supernatural." If we put all of this together, our working definition of mantra becomes "repeating a word or phrase that matters and that has seemingly mystical and supernatural powers."

It seems that a purpose is the perfect mantra. A purpose is a statement that not only matters, but that matters most. And, as you learned in the previous chapter, purpose holds a range of seemingly mystical and supernatural powers—from increasing courage and overcoming fear, to providing endurance in even the toughest of circumstances. It should come as no surprise, then, that using our purpose as a mantra during "self-talk" (repeating it in our heads) can have significant performance-enhancing effects.

There is widespread evidence that self-talk boosts performance. In particular, studies show that self-talk increases motivation and willingness to endure uncomfortable situations. Self-talk is most effective when what we tell ourselves is short, specific, and, most important, consistent. Thus, if your purpose is on the lengthy side, when using it as a self-talk strategy you may want to condense it into a few words that capture its essence. Self-talk is especially helpful in situations when our bodies and/or minds are telling us to quit, but we want to keep going. It helps us keep our cool and avoid amygdala hijack, or the emotional takeover of the brain that we discussed in Chapter 4. And, especially if the content of self-talk reflects a self-transcending purpose, it can empower us to do more than we ever thought possible.

As you might imagine, this strategy is quite common in athletics. Every athlete with whom we spoke in the process of writing this book told us that they use self-talk. During the final few miles of a marathon, for example, Olympic marathoner Desiree Linden told us that self-talk is as, if not more, important as hydration. But self-talk is a strategy that can be lifted out of athletics and put to great use in other fields, too. Regardless of what you are doing—whether you are using your body, mind, or soul—repeating a purpose-driven mantra during times of fear, pain, or apprehension can yield big benefits. Doing so grounds us, attenuates negative emotions, and quiets our ego, which as you learned in Chapter 8 loves nothing more than telling us to quit.

Although Merriam-Webster's dictionary may define the benefits of a mantra as mystical, by now you should know they are actually quite scientific.

Nightly Reflection

During the discussion of visual cues, we recommended that you stick your purpose on your bathroom mirror so you see it every morning to start your day. Coming full circle, we also think it's a good idea to reflect on your purpose every night. In particular, we encourage you to ask yourself: On a scale of 1 to 10 (with 10 being "completely" and 1 being "not at all"), did you live today with purpose? After making your ranking, spend just a minute or two reflecting on what you could have done differently to move closer to a 10. If you gave yourself a 10, reflect on what you did to get there. This short and simple act goes a long way toward helping you make the changes necessary to live in fuller alignment with your purpose, which as you already know improves performance in just about everything. While it's fine to go through this exercise in your head, research suggests that physically writing these reflections down enhances not only your performance but also your health.

"Expressive writing"—a type of journaling that involves exploring issues that are integral and foundational to our lives—has been shown to strengthen the cells in our immune systems. In addition, expressive writing is associated with declines in depression and anxiety, reduced blood pressure, fewer visits to the doctor, improved lung and liver function, and increases in positivity and social connectedness. Scientists speculate that expressive writing yields such profound results because it gives us a safe space to reflect on the issues that are most important to us. Many of us otherwise inhibit these thoughts and feelings, keeping them to ourselves. But as anyone who has kept deep feelings bottled up inside knows, doing so can cause a great deal of tension. Yet, at the same time, sharing them with others can also be a less-than-comfortable experience. By letting the words that reflect our deepest values and emotions pour out onto the page, we release tension and in doing so improve our health. In the words of University of Texas at Austin professor James Pennebaker, PhD, a pioneer of expressive writing research, "Standing back every now and then and evaluating where you are in life is really important." If anything epitomizes Pennebaker's definition of expressive writing, it's when we reflect on our purpose in an effort to determine how closely we lived in accordance with it.

A PURPOSE-DRIVEN LIFE

While reminding yourself of your purpose yields big benefits, what we really want is for you to act on it. There is nothing that enhances performance, vitality, and health like living on purpose. If you get only one thing out of this book, we hope it is this.

Once you've developed a purpose, do whatever it is you can to build a life that allows you fulfill it. The closer you can move to a 10—living completely in alignment with your purpose—the better, happier, and healthier you'll be. In the words of Ryan Hall, the fastest American marathon runner of all time, living out your purpose "is the best feeling in the world."

CONCLUSION

There is nothing more gratifying or fulfilling than setting a goal on the outer boundaries of what we think is possible, and then systematically pursuing it. In a paradoxical twist, we are often at our best when we wholly immerse ourselves in the process of getting better. All of the great performers you heard from in this book share the inability to be content. Even though they may be atop their respective fields, they remain fiercely driven to improve. We hope that you are inspired to adopt a similar mindset in your own pursuits.

Throughout this book, we've covered the key principles underlying healthy, sustainable peak performance:

- Stress + rest = growth

- The power of developing optimal routines and designing your day

- Purpose

While we hope that you've enjoyed reading, the real fun begins when you lift the ink off these pages and apply the principles in your own life.

Take note: None of the great performers that you heard from in this book followed an exact prescription. Rather, they took the performance principles and related practices and made them their own, adapting them to fit their unique styles and the specific demands of their activities. We encourage you to do the same.

To help get you started, we've summarized on the following pages the key practices that fall under each principle. Think of this as the base of a recipe that, over time, you'll make your own. As you do just that, we'd love to hear about your experience. Please send us your stories and learnings at info@peakperformance.email. We'll share these stories, along with the latest findings in performance science, in our newsletter, which you can subscribe to by visiting www.peakperformancebook.net. It is our hope that this book is just the beginning, and that we can create a community of individuals who share in common a desire to learn and improve.

FOR US, THIS BOOK project represented peak performance. Though it wasn't always easy, we did our best to practice what we preached. As we send you off on your own journey, we want to thank you for accompanying us on ours.

SYSTEMATICALLY GROW BY ALTERNATING BETWEEN STRESS AND REST

Stress Yourself

Seek out "just-manageable challenges" in areas of your life in which you want grow

- Just-manageable challenges are those that barely exceed your current abilities.

- If you feel fully in control, make the next challenge a bit harder.

- If you feel anxious or so aroused that you can't focus, dial things down a notch.

Cultivate deep focus and perfect practice

- Define a purpose and concrete objectives each time you set out to do meaningful work.

- Focus and concentrate deeply, even if doing so isn't always enjoyable.

- Remove distractors such as smartphones; remember that out of sight is truly out of mind.

- Do only one thing at a time. Next time you feel like multitasking, remind yourself that research shows it's not effective.

- Remember that quality trumps quantity.

Work in discrete blocks

- Divide your work into blocks of 50 to 90 minutes (this may vary by task). Start even smaller if you find yourself struggling to maintain attention.

- If deep-focus work is new to you, start with blocks as short as 10 to 15 minutes. As you cultivate a deep-focus practice, gradually increase the duration you go deep.

- For almost all activities, 2 hours should be the uppermost limit for a working block.

Nurture a growth or challenge mindset

- Keep in mind that how you view something fundamentally changes how your body responds to it.

- In situations when you feel the sensation of stress, remind yourself that this is your body's natural way of preparing for a challenge. Take a deep breath and channel the heightened arousal and sharper perception into the task at hand.

- Push yourself to view stress productively, and even to welcome it. You'll not only perform better but also improve your health.

Have the Courage to Rest

Grow your mindful muscle with meditation so that you can more easily choose rest

- Find a time when other distractions are minimized, such as first thing in the morning, after brushing your teeth, or before going to bed.

- Sit in a comfortable position and, ideally, in a quiet space.

- Set a timer so you aren't distracted by thoughts about the passage of time.

- Begin breathing deeply, in and out through your nose.

- Focus on nothing but your breath; when thoughts arise, notice them, but then let them go. Direct your focus back to the sensation of the breath.

- Start with just 1 minute and gradually increase duration, adding 30 to 45 seconds every few days.

- Frequency trumps duration. It's best to meditate daily, even if that means keeping individual sessions short.

Apply your growing mindful muscle in everyday life

- Have "calm conversations" during stressful periods; remember that you are separate from the emotions and sensations that you are experiencing.

- Realize when you want to "turn it off" and then *choose* to leave stress behind. Taking a few deep breaths helps because it activates the pre-frontal cortex, your brain's command-and-control center.

Take smart breaks and let your subconscious go to work

- When you are working on a strenuous task and hit an impasse, have the courage to step away.
  - Step away from whatever it is you were doing for at least 5 minutes.
  - The more stressful the task, the longer your break should be.
  - For really draining tasks, consider stepping away until the next morning.

- During your breaks, perform activities that demand little to no focus.
  - Go on a short walk.
  - Sit in nature.
  - Meditate.

- Recover socially.

- Listen to music.

- Take a shower.

- Do the dishes.

- You may have an "aha" moment of insight during your break. If you do, great. Even if you don't have an "aha" moment during your break, your subconscious mind is still at work. When you return to whatever it is you were doing, you'll be more likely to make progress.

Prioritize sleep

- Reframe sleep as something that is productive.

- Aim for at least 7 to 9 hours of sleep per night. For those doing intense physical activity, 10 hours is *not* too much.

- The best way to figure out the right amount of sleep for you is to spend 10 to 14 days going to sleep when you are tired and waking up without an alarm clock. Take the average sleep time. That's what you need.

- For a better night's sleep, follow these tips:

  - Ensure you expose yourself to natural (i.e., non-electric) light throughout the day. This will help you maintain a healthy circadian rhythm.

  - Exercise. Vigorous physical activity makes us tired. When we are tired, we sleep. But don't exercise too close to bedtime.

  - Limit caffeine intake, and phase it out completely 5 to 6 hours prior to your bedtime.

  - Only use your bed for sleep and sex. Not for eating, watching television, working on your laptop, or anything else. The one exception is reading a paper book prior to bed.

- Don't drink alcohol close to bedtime. Although alcohol can hasten the onset of sleep, it often disrupts the later and more important stages.

- Limit blue light exposure in the evening.

- Don't start working on hard, stressful activities—be they mental or physical—after dinner.

- If you struggle with a racing mind, try inserting a brief mindfulness meditation session prior to bed.

- When you feel yourself getting drowsy, don't fight it. Whatever you are doing can wait until the morning.

- Keep your room as dark as possible. If feasible, consider black-out blinds.

- Keep your smartphone OUT of the bedroom entirely. Not on silent. Out.

- Try taking a nap of 10 to 30 minutes to help restore energy and focus if you hit a mid-afternoon lull.

Take extended time off

- Regardless of the work you do, take at least one off-day every week.

- To the extent that you can, time your off-days and vacations strategically to follow periods of accumulated stress.

- The more you stress, the more you should rest.

- On both single off-days and extended vacations, truly disconnect from work. Unplug both physically and mentally and engage in activities that you find relaxing and restorative.

PRIME FOR PERFORMANCE

Optimize Your Routine

Develop warmup regimens for important activities/performances

- Determine what state of mind and body your performance demands.

- Develop a sequence of activities that puts your mind and body in that state.

- Be consistent: Use the same routine each and every time you engage in the activity to which it is linked.

- Remember the impact of mood on performance; positivity goes a long way.

Create "a place of your own"

- Find physical spaces to dedicate to unique activities.

- Surround yourself with objects that invite desired behaviors.

- Consistently work in that same place, using the same materials.

- Over time, your environment will enhance your productivity on a deep neurological level.

Condition yourself to perform

- Link key behaviors to specific cues and/or routines.

- Be consistent and frequent; execute the same cue/routine every time prior to the behavior to which it is paired.

- If possible, link key activities to the same context (e.g., time of day, physical environment, etc.).

- If your pursuit requires variable settings, develop portable cues/routines that can be executed anywhere (e.g., a deep-breathing routine, self-talk, etc.).

- Consistency is king. The best routine means nothing if you don't regularly practice it.

Design Your Day

Become a minimalist to be a maximalist

- Reflect on all the decisions that you make throughout a day.

- Identify ones that are unimportant, that "don't really matter" to you.

- To the extent that you can, automate those decisions that don't really matter. Common examples include decisions about:

  - Clothing

  - What to eat at meals

  - When to complete daily activities (e.g., always exercise at the same time of the day so you literally don't need to think about it)

  - Whether to attend social gatherings (It's not *always* a good idea, but during important periods of work, many great performers adopt a strict policy of saying no to social events)

- Don't devote brain power to gossip, politics, or worrying about what others think of you.

- Consider the second- and third-order effects (e.g., commute, financial pressures, etc.) of larger life decisions, such as where to live.

Match activities with energy levels

- Determine your chronotype (e.g., whether you are a morning lark or night owl).

- Design your day accordingly—be very intentional about when you schedule certain activities, matching the demands of the activity with your energy level.

- Protect the time during which you are most alert for "the most important work."

- Schedule less-demanding tasks during periods in which you are less alert.

- Don't fight fatigue! Rather, use this time for recovery and to generate creative ideas that you can act on during your next cycle of high energy and focus.

- Remember that working in alignment with your chronotype not only maximizes performance, it also ensures an appropriate balance between stress and rest.

Surround yourself wisely

- Recognize the enormous power of the people with whom you surround yourself.

- Do what you can to cultivate your own village of support so that you surround yourself with a culture of performance. Positive energy, motivation, and drive are all contagious.

- Remember that by being positive and showing motivation, you are not only helping yourself, you are also helping everyone else in your life.

- Don't put up with too much negativity or pessimism. A chain is only as strong as its weakest link.

Show up

- There is no replacement for showing up, day in and day out, to hone your craft.

- Remember that attitudes often follow behaviors; sometimes the best thing that you can do is to simply get started.

HARNESS THE POWER OF PURPOSE

Transcend Your "self"

Overcome your ego

- Remember that your "ego" or "self" or "central governor" serves as a protective mechanism that holds you back from reaching your true limits. When faced with great challenges, your ego is biologically programmed to shut you down, telling you to turn in the other direction.

- By focusing on a self-transcending purpose, or a reason for doing something beyond your self, you can override your ego and break through your self-imposed limits.

- To the extent you can, link your activities to a greater purpose. This way, when you are faced with formidable challenges and your mind is telling you to quit, you can ask yourself why you are doing it. If the answer is "for someone or something greater than myself," you'll be more likely to push onward.

- Thinking less about your self is one of the best ways to improve yourself.

Enhance your motivation

- Recall that you are constantly balancing perception of effort, or how hard something feels, with motivation. Thus, if you want to endure more effort, you may need to increase your motivation.

- To increase motivation, link your work to a greater purpose or cause.

- Not only will focusing on activities that help others make the world a better place, it will also help make you a better performer.

- Think about *why* you are doing what you are doing, especially when you are feeling fatigued.

Give back to avoid burnout

- Find opportunities to give back in the context of your work. These can be more intensive activities like coaching and mentoring, or less intensive acts like posting sincere advice in online forums.

- The only criteria is that the giving is closely linked to your work and that you give without the expectation of getting anything back.

- While giving is especially powerful for preventing and reversing burnout, you should still aim to avoid burnout by supporting stress with appropriate rest.

Develop and Harness Your Purpose

Develop your purpose using the exercises on pages 183 to 185

- Select your core values.
- Personalize your core values.
- Rank your core values.
- Write your purpose statement.

Strategically call upon your purpose

- Use visual cues to remind yourself of your purpose when you are most likely to need a boost.

- Develop a mantra based on your purpose and use it for self-talk when the going gets tough.

- Reflect on your purpose nightly (try using expressive writing). Think about how closely you lived in alignment with your purpose, striving to move closer to consistent alignment over time.

BIBLIOGRAPHY AND SOURCE NOTES

INTRODUCTION

Jim Clifton, *The Coming Jobs War* (New York: Gallup Press, 2011), 1-2.

Laura A. Pratt, PhD; Debra J. Brody, MPH; and Qiuping Gu, MD, PhD, "Antidepressant Use in Persons Aged 12 and Over: United States, 2005-2008," *NCHS Data Brief*, no. 7 (October 2011).

Matt Saccaro, "'I Think America is Out of Hand': The Shocking Numbers that Reveal Just How Burnt Out American Workers Are," *Salon*, June 29, 2015, http://www.salon.com/2015/06/29/i_think_america_is_out_of_hand_the _shocking_numbers_that_reveal_just_how_burnt_out_american_workers _are/.

Julie Bosman and Michael J. De La Merced, "Borders Files for Bankruptcy," *New York Times Dealbook*, February 16, 2011, http://dealbook.nytimes. com/2011/02/16/borders-files-for-bankruptcy/?_r=0.

Zeynep Tufekci, "The Machines Are Coming," *New York Times*, April 18, 2015, http://www.nytimes.com/2015/04/19/opinion/sunday/the-machines-are -coming.html?_r=0.

"An Open Letter: Research Priorities for Robust and Beneficial Artificial Intelligence," FutureOfLife.org, accessed November 11, 2015, http://futureof life.org/ai-open-letter/.

Rory Cellan-Jones, "Stephen Hawking Warns Artificial Intelligence Could End Mankind," *BBC*, December 2, 2014, http://www.bbc.com/news/technology -30290540.

Kevin Lynch "Introduction: 60 at 60," accessed: November 20, 2015, http://www .guinnessworldrecords.com/news/60at60/2015/8/introduction-393032

"Chronological Listing of U.S. Milers Who Have Broken 4:00 in the Mile," *Track & Field News*, last updated October 8, 2016, http://www.trackandfieldnews .com/index.php/archivemenu/13-lists/1476-tafn-us-sub-400-milers.

Andrew Powell-Morse, "The Historical Profile of the NBA Player: 1947-2015," *SeatSmart*, March 4, 2015, http://seatsmart.com/blog/history-of-the-nba -player/.

Addie Thomas, "Global Nutrition Supplements Market: History, Industry Growth, and Future Trends by PMR," *Nasdaq Globe Newswire*, January 27, 2015, http://globenewswire.com/news-release/2015/01/27/700276/10117198/en

/Global-Nutrition-and-Supplements-Market-History-Industry-Growth-and
-Future-Trends-by-PMR.html.

Marika Beale et al., "Examining the Enhancement Drink NeuroBliss®: Lack of Effect
on Mood and Memory in Late Adolescents," *Impulse: The Premier
Undergraduate Neuroscience Journal* (2014): 1-8, http://impulse.appstate.edu
/sites/impulse.appstate.edu/files/Beale%20et%20al%20%282%29.pdf.

Stephen V Faraone et al., "The Worldwide Prevalence of ADHD: Is It an American
Condition?," *World Psychiatry* 2, no. 2 (June 2003): 104-113.

"Attention-Deficit/Hyperactivity Disorder (ADHD)," Centers for Disease Control and
Prevention, last updated October 5, 2016, http://www.cdc.gov/ncbddd
/adhd/data.html.

A.D. DeSantis, E.M. Webb, and S.M. Noar, "Illicit Use of Prescription ADHD
Medications on a College Campus: A Multimethodological Approach," *Journal
of American College Health* 57, no. 3 (November–December 2008): 315-324.

Arianna Yanes, "Just Say Yes? The Rise of 'Study Drugs' in College," *CNN*, April 18,
2014, http://www.cnn.com/2014/04/17/health/adderall-college-students/.

Alan Schwarz, "Workers Seeking Productivity in a Pill are Abusing A.D.H.D. Drugs,"
New York Times, April 18, 2015, http://www.nytimes.com/2015/04/19/us
/workers-seeking-productivity-in-a-pill-are-abusing-adhd-drugs.html?_r=0.

Erik Parens, "A Symptom of Modern Life," Room for Debate, *New York Times*, April
21, 2015, http://www.nytimes.com/roomfordebate/2015/04/21/using
-adderall-to-get-ahead-not-to-fight-adhd/a-symptom-of-modern-life.

Olivier de Hon, Harm Kuipers, and Maarten van Bottenburg, "Prevalence of
Doping Use in Elite Sports: A Review of Numbers and Methods," *Sports
Medicine* 45, no. 1 (January 2015): 57-69.

Josie Feliz, "National Study: Teens Report Higher Use of Performance Enhancing
Substances," *Partnership for Drug-Free Kids*, July 22, 2014, http://www
.drugfree.org/newsroom/pats-2013-teens-report-higher-use-of-performance
-enhancing-substances.

"Anti-Doping," USA Triathlon, access date November 20, 2015, http://www
.usatriathlon.org/audience/athlete-resources/anti-doping.aspx.

David Epstein, "Everyone's Juicing," *ProPublica*, September 17, 2015, http://www
.propublica.org/article/raids-steroid-labs-suggest-market-for-steroids
-beyond-elite-athletes.

Deloitte University Press, *Global Human Capital Trends 2014*, accessed November
16, 2015, https://dupress.deloitte.com/dup-us-en/focus/human-capital
-trends/2014.html?icid=hp:ft:01.

LexisNexis, *The 2010 International Workplace Productivity Survey*, accessed
November 16, 2015, http://www.multivu.com/players/English/46619
-LexisNexis-International-Workplace-Productivity-Survey/.

Jada A. Graves and Katy Marquardt, "The Vanishing Lunch Break," *U.S. News & World Report*, October 9, 2013, http://money.usnews.com/money/careers /articles/2013/10/09/the-vanishing-lunch-break-2.

Daniel Hamermesh and Elena Stancanelli, "Americans Work Too Long (and Too Often at Strange Times)," *Vox*, September 29, 2014, http://www.voxeu.org /article/americans-work-long-and-strange-times.

Project: Time Off, *The Hidden Costs of Unused Leave*, accessed November 17, 2015, http://www.projecttimeoff.com/sites/default/files/PTO_HiddenCosts _Report.pdf.

Lydia Saad, "The '40-Hour' Workweek is Actually Longer—by Seven Hours," *Gallup*, August 29, 2014, http://www.gallup.com/poll/175286/hour -workweek-actually-longer-seven-hours.aspx.

Staples Business Advantage, *2015 Workplace Index*, accessed November 17, 2015, https://go.staplesadvantage.com/workplaceindex.

Ben Moshinsky, "Bank of America Intern's 5 a.m. E-Mail Before Death Worried Mom," *Bloomberg*, November 22, 2013, http://www.bloomberg.com/news /articles/2013-11-22/bank-of-america-staff-quizzed-as-coroner-probes -intern-s-death.

Jackie Wattles, "Goldman Sachs Bans Interns from Staying Overnight at the Office," *CNN Money*, June 17, 2015, http://money.cnn.com/2015/06/17 /news/companies/goldman-limit-intern-hours/.

D. Smith Bailey, "Burnout Harms Workers' Physical Health Through Many Pathways," *Monitor on Psychology* 37, no. 6 (June 2006): 11.

Shahm Martini et al., "Burnout Comparison Among Residents in Different Medical Specialties," *Academic Psychiatry* 28, no. 3 (September 2004): 240-242.

Carol Peckham, "Physician Burnout: It Just Keeps Getting Worse," *Medscape*, January 26, 2015, http://www.medscape.com/viewarticle/838437.

Joachim Bauer et al., "Correlation Between Burnout Syndrome and Psychological and Psychosomatic Symptoms Among Teachers," *International Archives of Occupational and Environmental Health* 79, no. 3 (March 2006): 199-204.

Ji Hye Yu, Su Jin Chae, and Ki Hong Chang, "The Relationship Among Self-Efficacy, Perfectionism, and Academic Burnous in Medical School Students," *Korean Journal of Medical Education* 28, no. 1 (March 2016): 49-55.

Mark McGuinness, "The Dark Side of Creativity: Burnout," *Lateral Action*, accessed November 17, 2015, http://lateralaction.com/articles/the-dark-side -of-creativity-burnout/.

Simon Kyaga, *Creativity and Psychopathology* (Stockholm: Karolinska Institutet, 2014).

Eystein Enoksen, "Drop-out Rate and Drop-out Reasons among Promising Norwegian Track and Field Athletes: A 25 Year Study," *Scandinavian Sports Studies Forum*, no. 2 (2011): 19-43.

Jeffrey B. Kreher, MD, and Jennifer B. Schwartz, MD, "Overtraining Syndrome," *Sports Health* 4, no. 2 (2012): 128-138.

W.P. Morgan et al., "Psychological Characterization of the Elite Female Distance Runner," *International Journal of Sports Medicine* 8, no. S2 (1987): 124-131.

John Raglin et al., "Training Practices and Staleness in 13–18-Year-Old Swimmers: A Cross-cultural Study," *Pediatric Exercise Science*, no. 12 (2000): 61-70.

CHAPTER 1

Matt Fitzgerald, "Deena Kastor's Comfort Zone," competitor.com, November 2, 2009, http://running.competitor.com/2009/11/training/deena-kastors -comfort-zone_6616.

Stephen Seiler, "What is Best Practice for Training Intensity and Duration Distribution in Endurance Athletes?," *International Journal of Sports Physiology and Performance*, no. 5 (2010): 276-291.

Mihaly Csikszentmihalyi, *Creativity: The Psychology of Discovery and Invention* (New York: HarperCollins Publishers, 1996): 21-127.

Roy F. Baumeister et al., "Ego Depletion: Is the Active Self a Limited Resource?," *Journal of Personality and Social Psychology* 74, no. 5 (1998): 1252-1265.

Mark Muraven, et al., "Self-Control as Limited Resource: Regulatory Depletion Problems," *Journal of Personality and Social Psychology* 74, no. 3: 774-789.

Dylan D. Wagner et al., "Self-Regulatory Depletion Enhances Neural Responses to Rewards and Impairs Top-Down Control," *Psychological Science* 24, no. 11 (November 2013): 2262-2271.

Malte Friese et al., "Suppressing Emotions Impairs Subsequent Stroop Performance and Reduces Prefrontal Brain Activation," *PLoS ONE* 8, no. 4 (April 2013): e60385.

Michael Inzlicht and Jennifer N. Gutsell, "Running on Empty: Neural Signals for Self-Control Failure," *Psychological Science* 18, no. 11 (2007): 933-937.

Kelly McGonigal, PhD, *The Willpower Instinct: How Self-Control Works, Why It Matters, and What You Can Do to Get More of It* (New York: Avery, 2012), 55-81.

Josh Waitzkin, *The Art of Learning: An Inner Journey to Optimal Performance* (New York: Free Press, 2007), 181-182.

CHAPTER 2

David G. Myers, *Psychology*, 6th ed. (Michigan: Worth Publishers, 2001), 604.

Manu Kapur, "Productive Failure in Learning the Concept of Variance," *Instructional Science* 40, no. 4 (July 2012): 651-672.

Kurt VanLehn et al., "Why Do Only Some Events Cause Learning During Human Tutoring?," *Cognition and Instruction* 21, no. 3 (2003): 209-249.

Daniel Kahneman, *Thinking, Fast and Slow* (New York: Farrar, Straus and Giroux, 2011), 3-31.

Ian A. McKenzie et al., "Motor Skill Learning Requires Active Central Myelination," *Science* 346, no. 6207 (October 17, 2014): 318-322.

CHAPTER 3

Frederick Reif and Sue Allen, "Cognition for Interpreting Scientific Concepts: A Study of Acceleration," *Cognition and Instruction* 9, no. 1 (1992): 1-44.

K. Anders Ericsson, "Deliberate Practice and the Acquisition and Maintenance of Expert Performance Medicine and Related Domains," *Academic Medicine* 79, no. S10 (October 2004): S70-81.

Robyn M. Dawes, *House of Cards: Psychology and Psychotherapy Built on Myth* (New York: Free Press, 1994), 55-56.

Richard Gawel, "The Use of Language by Trained and Untrained Experienced Wine Tasters," *Journal of Sensory Studies* 12, no. 4 (December 1997): 267-284; D. Valentin et al., "What's in a Wine Name? When and Why Do Wine Experts Perform Better than Novices?" *Abstracts of the Psychonomic Society* 5 (2000): 36.

K. Anders Ericsson, Ralf Th. Krampe, and Clemens Tesch-Romer, "The Role of Deliberate Practice in the Acquisition of Expert Performance," *Psychological Review* 100, no. 3 (1993): 363-406.

K. Anders Ericsson, "The Influence of Experience and Deliberate Practice on the Development of Superior Expert Performance," in *The Cambridge Handbook of Expertise and Expert Performance*, ed. K. Anders Ericsson et al. (New York: Cambridge University Press, 2006), 685-706.

K. Anders Ericsson, "The Acquisition of Expert Performance: An Introduction to Some of the Issues," in *The Road to Excellence: The Acquisition of Expert Performance in the Arts and Sciences, Sports, and Games*, ed. K. Anders Ericsson (Mahwah, NJ: Lawrence Erlbaum Associates, Inc., Publishers, 1996), 1-50; K. Anders Ericsson and A.C. Lehmann, "Expert and Exceptional Performance: Evidence of Maximal Adaption to Task Constraints," *Annual Review of Psychology* 47 (1996): 273-305.

Christina Grape et al., "Does Singing Promote Well-Being? An Empirical Study of Professional and Amateur Singers During a Singing Lesson," *Integrative Physiological & Behavioral Science* 38, no. 1 (January 2002): 65-74.

J.M. Watson and D.L. Strayer, "Supertaskers: Profiles in Extraordinary Multitasking Ability," *Psychonomic Bulletin & Review* 17, no. 4 (August 2010): 479-485.

Gisela Telis, "Multitasking Splits the Brain," *Science*, April 15, 2010, http://www.sciencemag.org/news/2010/04/multitasking-splits-brain.

Joshua S. Rubinstein, David E. Meyer, and Jeffrey E. Evans, "Executive Control of Cognitive Processes in Task Switching," *Journal of Experimental Psychology: Human Perception and Performance* 27, no. 4 (2001): 763-797.

"Injury Prevention & Control: Motor Vehicle Safety," Centers for Disease Control and Prevention, last updated March 7, 2016, http://www.cdc.gov/motor vehiclesafety/distracted_driving/.

Patrick Anselme and Mike J.F. Robinson, "What Motivates Gambling Behavior? Insight into Dopamine's Role," *Frontiers in Behavioral Neuroscience* 7 (2013): 182.

Michelle Drouin, Daren H. Kaiser, and Daniel A. Miller, "Phantom Vibrations among Undergraduates: Prevalence and Associated Psychological Characteristics," *Computers in Human Behavior* 28, no. 4 (July 2012): 1490-1496.

Justin Worland, "How Your Cell Phone Distracts You Even When You're Not Using It," *Time,* December 4, 2014, http://time.com/3616383/cell-phone-distraction/.

Walter Mischel, *The Marshmallow Test: Mastering Self-Control* (New York: Little, Brown and Company, 2014): 233-273.

K. Anders Ericsson, "The Path to Expert Golf Performance: Insights from the Masters on How to Improve Performance by Deliberate Practice," in *Optimising Performance in Golf,* ed. Patrick R. Thomas (Brisbane, Australia: Australian Academic Press, 2001), 1-57; K. Anders Ericsson, "Development of Elite Performance and Deliberate Practice: An Update From the Perspective of the Expert Performance Approach," in *Expert Performance in Sports: Advances in Research on Sport Expertise,* ed. Janet L. Starkes and K. Anders Ericsson (Champaign, IL: Human Kinetics, 2003), 49-81.

Julia Gifford, "The Secret of the 10% Most Productive People? Breaking!," *DeskTime,* August 20, 2014, http://blog.desktime.com/2014/08/20/the-secret-of-the -10-most-productive-people-breaking/.

Awwad J. Dababneh, Naomi Swanson, and Richard L. Shell, "Impact of Added Rest Breaks on the Productivity and Well Being of Workers," *Ergonomics* 44, no. 2 (2001): 164-174.

P.S. Tiwari and L.P. Gite, "Evaluation of Work-Rest Schedules During Operation of a Rotary Power Tiller," *International Journal of Industrial Ergonomics* 36, no. 3 (March 2006): 203-210.

Wolfram Boucsein and Michael Thum, "Design of Work/Rest Schedules for Computer Work Based on Psychophysiological Recovery Measures," *International Journal of Industrial Ergonomics* 20, no. 1 (July 1997): 51-57.

Traci L. Galinsky et al., "A Field Study of Supplementary Rest Breaks for Data-Entry Operators," *Ergonomics* 43, no. 5 (2000): 622-638.

A.J. Crum et al., "Mind Over Milkshakes: Mindsets, Not Just Nutrients, Determine Ghrelin Response," *Health Psychology* 30, no. 4 (July 2011): 424-429.

Lisa S. Blackwell, Kali H. Trzesniewski, and Carol Sorich Dweck, "Implicit Theories of Intelligence Predict Achievement Across an Adolescent Transition: A

Longitudinal Study and an Intervention," *Child Development* 78, no. 1 (January/February 2007): 246-263.

Abiola Keller et al., "Does the Perception that Stress Affects Health Matter? The Association with Health and Mortality," *Healthy Psychology* 31, no. 5 (September 2012): 677-684.

Lee J Moore, et al., "The effect of challenge and threat states on performance: An examination of potential mechanisms," *Psychophysiology* 49, no. 10 (October 2012): 1417-1425.

Alia K. Crum, Peter Salovey, and Shawn Achor, "Rethinking Stress: The Role of Mindsets in Determining the Stress Response," *Journal of Personality and Social Psychology* 104, no. 4 (April 2013): 716-733.

Graham Jones, Sheldon Hanton, and Austin Swain, "Intensity and Interpretation of Anxiety Symptoms in Elite and Non-Elite Sports Performers," *Personality and Individual Differences* 17, no. 5 (November 1994): 657-663.

Brad Stulberg, "Should I Give Whitewater Kayaking a Try?," *Outside*, November 9, 2015, https://www.outsideonline.com/2034356/should-i-give-whitewater-kayaking-try.

CHAPTER 4

Sara W. Lazar et al., "Meditation Experience is Associated with Increased Cortical Thickness," *Neuroreport* 16, no. 17 (November 28, 2005): 1893-1897.

Amy F.T. Arnsten, "Stress Signalling Pathways that Impair Prefrontal Cortex Structure and Function," *Nature Reviews Neuroscience* 10, no. 6 (June 2009): 410-422.

Antoine Lutz et al., "Altered Anterior Insula Activation During Anticipation and Experience of Painful Stimuli in Expert Meditators," *NeuroImage* 64 (January 1, 2013): 538-546.

Stephen Seiler, Olav Haugen, and Erin Kuffel, "Autonomic Recovery after Exercise in Trained Athletes: Intensity and Duration Effects," *Medicine & Science in Sports & Exercise* 39, no. 8 (August 2007): 1366-1373.

M. Tudor, L. Tudor, and K.I. Tudor, "Hans Berger (1873-1941)—The History of Electroencephalography," *Acta Medica Croatica* 59, no. 4 (2005): 307-313.

Susan Whitfield-Gabrieli and Judith M. Ford, "Default Mode Network Activity and Connectivity in Psychopathology," *Annual Review of Clinical Psychology* 8 (April 2012): 49-76.

Marcus E. Raichle et al., "A Default Mode of Brain Function," *Proceeding of the National Academy of Sciences of the United States of America* 98, no. 2 (January 16, 2001): 676-682.

Mason Currey, *Daily Rituals: How Artists Work* (New York: Knopf, 2013), 120-121.

Frank Stewart, *A Natural History of Nature Writing* (Island Press, 1994), 4.

Jonathan Smallwood and Jonathan W. Schooler, "The Science of Mind Wandering: Empirically Navigating the Stream of Consciousness," *Annual Review of Psychology* 66 (January 2015): 487-518.

Simone M. Ritter and Ap Dijksterhuis, "Creativity—The Unconscious Foundations of the Incubation Period," *Frontiers in Human Neuroscience* 8 (2014): 215.

Shantanu P. Jadhav et al., "Awake Hippocampal Sharp-Wave Ripples Support Spatial Memory," *Science* 336, no. 6087 (June 15, 2012): 1454-1458.

CHAPTER 5

Steven Pressfield, *The War of Art: Winning the Inner Creative Battle* (New York: Rugged Land, LLC, 2002), 125.

Marily Oppezzo and Daniel L. Schwartz, "Give Your Ideas Some Legs: The Positive Effect of Walking on Creative Thinking," *Journal of Experimental Psychology: Learning, Memory, and Cognition* 40, no. 4 (2014): 1142-1152.

Patti Neighmond, "Walking 2 Minutes an Hour Boosts Health, But It's No Panacea," *NPR*, May 1, 2015, http://www.npr.org/sections/health-shots/2015/05/01/403523463/two-minutes-of-walking-an-hour-boosts -health-but-its-no-panacea; Srinivasan Beddhu et al., "Light-Intensity Physical Activities and Mortality in the United States General Population and CKD Subpopulation," *Clinical Journal of the American Society of Nephrology* 10 (July 2015): 1-9.

Marc G. Berman, John Jonides, and Stephen Kaplan, "The Cognitive Benefits of Interacting with Nature," *Psychological Science* 19, no. 12 (2008): 1207-1212.

J.E. Stellar, "Positive Affect and Markers of Inflammation: Discrete Positive Emotions Predict Lower Levels of Inflammatory Cytokines," *Emotion* 15, no. 2 (April 2015): 129-133.

Lorenzo S. Colzato et al., "Prior Meditation Practice Modulates Performance and Strategy Use in Convergent- and Divergent-Thinking Problems," *Mindfulness* (2014): 1-7.

C.J. Cook and B.T. Crewther, "The Social Environment During a Post-Match Video Presentation Affects the Hormonal Responses and Playing Performance in Professional Male Athletes," *Physiology & Behavior* 130 (May 10, 2014): 170-175.

Brad Stulberg, "Use Your Mind to Restore Your Body After a Run," *Runner's World*, June 28, 2016, http://www.runnersworld.com/recovery/use-your-mind-to-restore -your-body-after-a-run.

Jeffrey M. Jones, "In U.S., 40% Get Less than Recommended Amount of Sleep," *Gallup*, December 19, 2013, http://www.gallup.com/poll/166553/less -recommended-amount-sleep.aspx.

Maria Konnikova, "Why Can't We Fall Asleep?," *The New Yorker*, July 7, 2015, http://www.newyorker.com/science/maria-konnikova/why-cant-we-fall-asleep.

Anne-Marie Chang et al., "Evening Use of Light-Emitting eReaders Negatively Affects Sleep, Circadian Timing, and Next-Morning Alertness," *Proceeding of the National Academy of Sciences of the United States of America* 112, no. 4 (January 27, 2015): 1232-1237.

Maria Konnikova, "The Work We Do While We Sleep," *The New Yorker*, July 8, 2015, http://www.newyorker.com/science/maria-konnikova/why-we-sleep.

Erin J. Wamsley, PhD, and Robert Stickgold, PhD, "Memory, Sleep and Dreaming: Experiencing Consolidation," *Sleep Medicine Clinics* 6, no. 1 (March 2011): 97-108.

S. Groch et al., "The Role of REM Sleep in the Processing of Emotional Memories: Evidence from Behavior and Event-Related Potentials," *Neurobiology of Learning and Memory* 99 (January 2013): 1-9.

Matthew P. Walker and Els van der Helm, "Overnight Therapy? The Role of Sleep in Emotional Brain Processing," *Psychological Bulletin* 135, no. 5 (September 2009): 731-748.

June J. Pilcher et al., "Interactions Between Sleep Habits and Self-Control," *Frontiers in Human Neuroscience* (May 11, 2015).

Gary Wittert, "The Relationship Between Sleep Disorders and Testosterone in Men," *Asian Journal of Andrology* 16, no. 2 (March-April 2014): 262-265.

P.T. Res, "Protein Ingestion Before Sleep Improves Postexercise Overnight Recovery," *Medicine & Science in Sports & Exercise* 44, no. 8 (August 2012): 1560-1569.

Cheri D. Mah et al., "The Effects of Sleep Extension on the Athletic Performance of Collegiate Basketball Players," *Sleep* 34, no. 7 (July 1, 2011): 943-950.

Kathleen McCann, "Ongoing Study Continues to Show that Extra Sleep Improves Athletic Performance," *American Academy of Sleep Medicine*, June 4, 2008, http://www.aasmnet.org/Articles.aspx?id=954.

Mark R. Rosekind et al., "Alertness Management: Strategic Naps in Operational Settings," *Journal of Sleep Research* 4, no. 2 (1995) 62-66.

Michael J. Breus, PhD, "Nap vs. Caffeine vs. More Nighttime Sleep?," *Psychology Today*, July 20, 2009, https://www.psychologytoday.com/blog/sleep -newzzz/200907/nap-vs-caffeine-vs-more-nighttime-sleep.

Clifford B. Saper, Thomas C. Chou, and Thomas E. Scammell, "The Sleep Switch: Hypothalamic Control of Sleep and Wakefulness," *Trends in Neurosciences* 24, no. 12 (December 1, 2001): 726-731.

"Sleep Hygiene Tips," Centers for Disease Control and Prevention, December 10, 2014, http://www.cdc.gov/sleep/about_sleep/sleep_hygiene.html.

"What is Sleep Hygiene?," National Sleep Foundation, accessed November 17, 2015, https://sleepfoundation.org/ask-the-expert/sleep-hygiene.

"Sleep Hygiene Tips," American Sleep Association, accessed November 17, 2015, https://www.sleepassociation.org/patients-general-public/insomnia /sleep-hygiene-tips/.

Scott Cacciola, "The Secret to Running: Not Running," *The Wall Street Journal*, September 20, 2012, http://www.wsj.com/articles/SB1000087239639044 40324045780062740107 45406.

Carmen Binnewies, Sabine Sonnentag, and Eva J. Mojza, "Daily Performance at Work: Feeling Recovered in the Morning as a Predictor of Day-Level Job Performance," *Journal of Organizational Behavior* 30, no. 1 (2009): 67-93.

Carmen Binnewies, Sabine Sonnentag, and Eva J. Mojza, "Recovery During the Weekend and Fluctuations in Weekly Job Performance: A Week-Level Study Examining Intra-Individual Relationships," *Journal of Occupational and Organizational Psychology* 83, no. 2 (June 2010): 419-441.

Jessica de Bloom, *How Do Vacations Affect Workers' Health and Well-Being?* (Oisterwijk, Netherlands: Uitgeverij BOXPress, 2012).

Dalia Etzion, "Annual Vacation: Duration of Relief from Job Stressors and Burnout," *Anxiety, Stress, & Coping* 16, no. 2 (2003): 213-226.

Leslie A. Perlow and Jessica L. Porter, "Making Time Off Predictable—and Required," *Harvard Business Review*, October 2009, https://hbr.org /2009/10/making-time-off-predictable-and-required.

CHAPTER 6

Kim Constantinesco, "Olympic Hopeful and Filmmaker Alexis Pappas Churns Miles and Words for the Perfect Mix," *Purpose2Play*, December 17, 2015, http://purpose2play.com/olympic-hopeful-and-filmmaker-alexi-pappas -churns-miles-and-words-for-the-perfect-mix/.

John Kounious and Mark Beeman, "Aha! The Cognitive Neuroscience of Insight," *Current Directions in Psychological Science* 18 (2009): 210-216.

Sheena Lewis, Mira Dontcheva, and Elizabeth Gerber, "Affective Computational Priming and Creativity," *CHI 2011 Conference on Human Factors in Computing Systems* (2011).

Anthony Blanchfield, James Hardy, and Samuele Marcora, "Non-Conscious Visual Cues Related to Affect and Action Alter Perception of Effort and Endurance Performance," *Frontiers in Human Neuroscience* 8 (December 11, 2014): 967.

Travis Proulx and Steven J. Heine, "Connections from Kafka: Exposure to Meaning Threats Improves Implicit Learning of an Artificial Grammar," *Psychological Science* 20, no. 9 (September 2009): 1125-1131.

Stephen King, *On Writing: A Memoir of the Craft* (New York: Scribner, 2000), 155.

Silvano Zipoli Caiani, "Extending the Notion of Affordance," *Phenomenology and the Cognitive Sciences* 13, no. 2 (June 2014): 275-293.

Mihaly Csikszentmihalyi, *The Evolving Self: A Psychology for the Third Millennium* (New York: HarperCollins Publishers, Inc., 1993), 139-141.

Mason Currey, *Daily Rituals: How Artists Work* (New York: Knopf, 2013), 120-121.

A.M. Graybiel, "Habits, Rituals, and the Evaluative Brain," *Annual Review of Neuroscience* 31 (2008): 359-387.

O. Beauchet, "Testosterone and Cognitive Function: Current Clinical Evidence of a Relationship," *European Journal of Endocrinology* 155, no. 6 (December 2006): 773-781.

CHAPTER 7

Drake Baer, "The Scientific Reason Why Barack Obama and Mark Zuckerberg Wear the Same Outfit Every Day," *Business Insider*, April 28, 2015, http://www.businessinsider.com/barack-obama-mark-zuckerberg-wear-the-same-outfit-2015-4.

Michael Lewis, "Obama's Way," *Vanity Fair*, October 2012, http://www.vanityfair.com/news/2012/10/michael-lewis-profile-barack-obama.

Neil Vidmar, "The Psychology of Trial Judging," *Current Directions in Psychological Science* 20 (2011): 58-62.

Ed Yong, "Justice is Served, But More So After Lunch: How Food-Breaks Sway the Decisions of Judges," *Discover*, April 11, 2011, http://blogs.discovermagazine.com/notrocketscience/2011/04/11/justice-is-served-but-more-so-after-lunch-how-food-breaks-sway-the-decisions-of-judges/#.VpLKhvHer40.

Nicholas Bakalar, "Doctors and Decision Fatigue," *New York Times*, October 27, 2014, http://well.blogs.nytimes.com/2014/10/27/doctors-and-decision-fatigue/?_r=0.

Kathleen D. Vohs et al., "Making Choices Impairs Subsequent Self-Control: A Limited-Resource Account of Decision Making, Self-Regulation, and Active Initiative," *Journal of Personality and Social Psychology* 94, no. 5 (2008): 883–898.

Joseph Tzelgov, "Automaticity and Processing Without Awareness," *Psyche* 5, no. 3 (April 1999).

Till Roenneberg, *Internal Time: Chronotypes, Social Jet Lag, and Why You're So Tired* (Cologne, Germany: DuMont Buchverlag, 2010).

Brigitte M. Kudielka et al., "Morningness and Eveningness: The Free Cortisol Rise after Awakening in 'Early Birds' and 'Night Owls,'" *Biological Psychology* 72, no. 2 (May 2006): 141-146.

J.A. Horne and O. Ostberg, "A Self-Assessment Questionnaire to Determine Morningness-Eveningness in Human Circadian Rhythms," *International Journal of Chronobiology* 4, no. 2 (1976): 97-110.

Mareike B. Wieth and Rose T. Zacks, "Time of Day Effects on Problem Solving: When the Non-Optimal is Optimal," *Thinking & Reasoning* 17, no. 4 (2011): 387-401.

Scott E. Carrell, Mark Hoekstra, and James E. West, "Is Poor Fitness Contagious? Evidence from Randomly Assigned Friends," *Journal of Public Economics* 95 (August 2011): 657-663.

Ron Friedman et al., "Motivational Synchronicity: Priming Motivational Orientations with Observations of Others' Behaviors," *Motivation and Emotion* (March 2010): 34-8. doi: 10.1007/s11031-009-9151-3.

Paula M. Niedenthal, "Embodying Emotion," *Science* 316, no. 5827 (May 18, 2007): 1002-1005.

Philip L. Jackson, Andrew N. Meltzoff, and Jean Decety, "How Do We Perceive the Pain of Others? A Window into the Neural Processes Involved in Empathy," *Neurolmage* 24, no. 3 (February 1, 2005): 771-779.

Emma Seppälä, *The Happiness Track: How to Apply the Science of Happiness to Accelerate Your Success* (New York: HarperCollins Publishers, 2016), 162

Nicholas A. Christakis, MD, PhD, MPH, and James H. Fowler, PhD, "The Spread of Obesity in a Large Social Network over 32 Years," *The New England Journal of Medicine* 357 (2007): 370-379.

Nicholas A. Christakis, MD, PhD, MPH, and James H. Fowler, PhD, "Quitting in Droves: Collective Dynamics of Smoking Behavior in a Large Social Network," *The New England Journal of Medicine* 358, no. 21 (May 22, 2008): 2249-2258.

James Clear, "What is Actually Required for Success?," *James Clear (blog)*, accessed December 13, 2015, http://jamesclear.com/required-for-success.

Jocelyn K. Glei and Scott Belsky, *Manage Your Day-to-Day: Build Your Routine, Find Your Focus, and Sharpen Your Mind* (Amazon Publishing, 2013), 103.

CHAPTER 8

Alexis Huicochea, "Man Lifts Car Off Pinned Cyclist," Tuscon.com, July 28, 2006, http://tucson.com/news/local/crime/article_e7f04bbd-309b-5c7e-808d-1907d91517ac.html.

Julie Halpert, "On Purpose," *Michigan Today*, March 5, 2014, http://michigantoday.umich.edu/on-purpose/.

T.D. Noakes, "Time to Move Beyond a Brainless Exercise Physiology: The Evidence for Complex Regulation of Human Exercise Performance," *Applied Physiology, Nutrition, and Metabolism* 36, no. 1 (February 2011): 23-35.

T.D. Noakes, "J.B. Wolffe Memoiral Lecture. Challenging beliefs: ex Africa semper aliquid novi," *Medicine & Science in Sports & Exercise* 29, no. 5 (May 1997): 571-590.

Brad Stulberg, "What's the Point?," *Blue Ridge Outdoors Magazine*, July 22, 2015, http://www.blueridgeoutdoors.com/go-outside/whats-the-point/.

Emily B. Falk et al., "Self-Affirmation Alters the Brain's Response to Health Messages and Subsequent Behavior Change," *Proceedings of the National Academy of Sciences of the United States of America* 112, no. 7 (February 17, 2015): 1977-1982.

Stephen E. Humphrey, Jennifer D. Nahrgang, and Frederick P. Morgeson, "Integrating Motivational, Social, and Contextual Work Design Features: A Meta-Analytic Summary and Theoretical Extension of the Work Design Literature," *Journal of Applied Psychology* 92, no. 5 (September 2007): 1332-1356.

T.D. Shanafelt et al., "Career Fit and Burnout Among Academic Faculty," *Archives of Internal Medicine* 169, no. 10 (May 25, 2009): 990-995.

P.R. Harris et al., "Self-Affirmation Reduces Smokers' Defensiveness to Graphic On-Pack Cigarette Warning Labels," *Health Psychology* 26, no. 4 (July 2007): 437-446.

A.M. Grant and D.A. Hofmann, "It's Not All About Me: Motivating Hand Hygiene Among Health Care Professionals by Focusing on Patients," *Psychological Science* 22, no. 12 (December 2011): 1494-1499.

Adam Grant, "How Customers Can Rally Your Troops," *Harvard Business Review*, June 2011, https://hbr.org/2011/06/how-customers-can-rally-your-troops.

Samuele M. Marcora, "Do We Really Need a Central Governor to Explain Brain Regulation of Exercise Performance?," *European Journal of Applied Physiology* 104 (2008): 929-931.

Daniel Pink, *Drive: The Surprising Truth About What Motivates Us* (New York: Riverhead Books, 2012): 145.

David S. Yeager et al., "Boring But Important: A Self-Transcendent Purpose for Learning Fosters Academic Self-Regulation," *Journal of Personality and Social Psychology* 107, no. 4 (October 2014): 559-580.

Viktor Frankl, *Man's Search for Meaning* (Boston: Beacon Press, 2006), 80.

Shelley E. Taylor, "Tend and Befriend Theory," in *Handbook of Theories of Social Psychology*, ed. Paul A.M. van Lange, Arie W. Kruglanski, and E. Tory Higgins (London: Sage Publications, 2012).

David Conrad and Yvonne Kellar-Guenther, "Compassion Fatigue, Burnout, and Compassion Satisfaction among Colorado Child Protection Workers," *Child Abuse & Neglect* 30, no. 10 (October 2006): 1071-1080.

Adam M. Grant, *Give and Take: Why Helping Others Drives Our Success* (New York: Viking, 2013), 166.

Brad Stulberg, "The Cure for Fitness Burnout," *Men's Fitness*, October 15, 2014, http://www.mensfitness.com/training/pro-tips/cure-fitness-burnout.

CHAPTER 9

Anthony Blanchfield, James Hardy, and Samuele Marcora, "Non-Conscious Visual Cues Related to Affect and Action Alter Perception of Effort and Endurance Performance," *Frontiers in Human Neuroscience* 8 (December 11, 2014): 967.

Antonis Hatzigeorgiadis, Nikos Zourbanos, Evangelos Galanis and Yiannis Theodorakis, "Self-Talk and Sports Performance: A Meta-Analysis," *Perspectives on Psychological Science* 6, no. 4 (July 2011): 348-56.

Karen A. Baikie and Kay Wilhelm, "Emotional and Physical Health Benefits of Expressive Writing," *Advances in Psychiatric Treatment* 11, no. 5 (August 2005): 338-46.

ACKNOWLEDGMENTS

Writing this book was the ultimate team effort, not only between the two of us but also among so many other individuals who contributed in their own unique way. If you enjoyed *Peak Performance*, please join us in a moment of gratitude for the following people. Their imprint is all over the pages that you just read.

First and foremost, we want to thank our core team, without whom this book would still be in our heads instead of on paper. To Caitlin Stulberg, an unbelievable wife to one of us and an unbelievable editor to both of us. We finished the manuscript in under 3 months, and many people asked how we worked so fast. The answer is Caitlin. Caitlin turned around chapter-by-chapter edits faster than any professional with whom we've ever worked, and that's on top of her day job as an attorney. Every page of this book is better because of her—and not just because of her endless revisions, but even more so because of her unending support.

To our agent, Ted Weinstein, who took a shot on two young writers with little experience. Ted was instrumental in shaping the proposal, and thus the book. He embodies professionalism, and is a pleasure to work with and, perhaps most important, wonderful to learn from.

To the wonderful team at Rodale Books, including Aly Mostel and Angie Giammarino. And in particular our editor, Mark Weinstein, who believed in the concept for this book right from the start. Mark gave us the freedom to write the book that we wanted to write, and then he made it better. There's nothing more an author can ask for from an editor.

We also want to thank the readers of our early drafts, whose feedback improved this book immensely. These individuals took the time and energy to read the manuscript when it still lived in multiple Microsoft Word documents. Each one of them offered valuable input in hours of phone, Skype, and coffee-shop conversations. Thanks are in order to Sarah Baum, Mark Davies, Cally Macumber, Jonathan Marcus, Alan McClain, Hillary Montgomery, Alan Penskar, Melissa Stern, Eric Stulberg, Linda Stulberg, Phoebe Wright, and the members of the 2015 University of Houston cross country team (Caleb Beacham, Nikita Prasad, Mackenzie Ilari, Cam Laverty, Maria Gonzales, Rick Hawley, Kody Anderson, Jennifer Dunlap, Matt Parmley, Justin Barrett, Gabe Lara, Brian Barraza, Meredith Sorensen, GJ Reyna, and Trevor Walker). An extra special thanks are in order to Emily Magness, who demonstrated that she is the far better writer in the Magness family. Her edits and critique were an invaluable addition to the book.

We'd be remiss not to mention our mentors, who encouraged us to write this book and whose collective impression on us over the years shaped its message. We are fortunate to have lifelong teachers, and we are blessed to be surrounded by a circle of wisdom, kindness, and caring. A special thanks to David Epstein, Mario Fraioli, Vern Gambetta, Adam Grant, Bruce Grierson, Alex Hutchinson, Mike Joyner, Bob Kocher, and Kelly McGonigal.

Thanks are also in order to the publications to which we regularly contribute, including *Blue Ridge Outdoors* (in particular, Brad's editor Will Harlan), *New York* magazine (in particular, Brad's editor Melissa Dahl), *Outside* magazine (in particular, Brad's editors Erin Beresini, Meaghen Brown, and Wesley Judd), *Running Times* (in particular, Steve's editors Jonathan Beverly, Scott Douglas, and Erin Strout), and *Runner's World* (in particular, Brad's editors, Katie Neitz and Meghan Kita). An additional thanks to *Outside* magazine, *New York* magazine, and *Runner's World*, where some of the stories and insights in this book first appeared in Brad's columns. It's truly an honor to regularly write for such classy publications.

And, of course, thanks to all the great performers whose stories we shared in this book. While there are far too many to list individually, we do want to recognize a few individuals with whom we became especially close

>

during the reporting process. These stars went above and beyond to invite us into their lives: Emil Alzamora, Matt Billingslea, Matt Dixon, Megan Gaurnier, David Goss, Dave Hamilton, Mike Joyner, Bob Kocher, Jennifer Pharr Davis, Brandon Rennels, Darren Smith, and Vic Strecher.

Finally, thanks to the members of our families, who have always supported us in achieving our own individual Peak Performance. Without them, none of this would be possible. Caitlin. Linda and Bob Stulberg. Eric Stulberg. Lois Stulberg. Bob and Elaine Appel. Randee and Bob Bloom. William and Elizabeth Magness. Phillip and Emily Magness.

ABOUT THE AUTHORS

BRAD STULBERG writes about health and the science of human performance. He is a columnist with *Outside* magazine and *New York* magazine and has also written for *Forbes*, *NPR*, the *Los Angeles Times*, *Runner's World*, and *The Harvard Public Health Review*. Brad is widely known for his ability to merge the latest science with compelling personal stories, offering readers practical insights that they can apply in their own lives.

Previously, Brad worked as a consultant for McKinsey & Company, where he counseled some of the world's top executives on a broad range of issues. He is an avid athlete and outdoor enthusiast. Brad lives in Northern California with his wife, Caitlin, and their two cats. Follow Brad on Twitter @Bstulberg.

© Drevan Anderson-Kaapa

STEVE MAGNESS is a coach to some of the top distance runners in the world, having coached numerous athletes to the Olympic Trials, World Championship teams, and the Olympics. He currently coaches at the University of Houston.

Known widely for his integration of science and practice, Steve has been on the forefront of innovation in sport. He serves as an adjunct professor of strength and conditioning at St. Mary's University and has been a featured expert in *Runner's World*, the *New York Times*, the *New Yorker, BBC*, the *Wall Street Journal,* and *ESPN The Magazine.* His first book, *The Science of Running,* was published in 2014. In his own running, Steve ran a 4:01 mile in high school. He lives in Houston, Texas. Follow Steve on Twitter @SteveMagness.

To learn more, visit www.peakperformancebook.net.

INDEX

Underscored page references indicate sidebars. **Boldface** references indicate illustrations.